RITUALS
FOR WORK

RITUALS FOR WORK

50 WAYS TO CREATE ENGAGEMENT, SHARED PURPOSE
AND A CULTURE THAT CAN ADAPT TO CHANGE

Kursat Ozenc, Ph.D.
Margaret Hagan, Ph.D.

WILEY

We dedicate this book to our families, and in particular
Aliye, Mehmet, and Selcen.

Contents

PART THREE
Designing Rituals with and for Your Teams

What Kinds of Ritual Do You Need?

Individual

Chapter 3

creATivity + iNNoVAtion

+ Fire up the right brain
+ Bring dead projects to life
+ Start building things quickly

Chapter 4

PERFoRMANCe AND FLOW

+ Make your focus tangible
+ Eliminate distractions for deep work
+ Manage your emotions in a high stakes situation
+ Create a sense of control and boost confidence

Chapter 5

CoNFLict & ReSilieNCe

+ Encourage team members to avoid clashes
+ Decrease anxiety before feedback sessions
+ Repair deteriorating relationships

Chapter 6

CoMMUNity

+ Create an identity to foster a sense of belonging
+ Increase empathy among team members
+ Share personal histories to increase bonding

Chapter 7

CHANGE + TrANSitioN

+ Welcome a new hire into the organization
+ Celebrate the start of "real" work
+ Deal with career changes

Team

Org

+ Encourage lateral thinking
+ Giving license to risk and fail
+ Inspire the team with idea building
+ Meet people where they are struggling

+ Develop solutions for recurring issues
+ Create a culture of ideation and controlled risk-taking
+ Encourage everyone to share their skills

+ Rescue the team from distractions
+ Move stalled projects forward
+ Recognize the purpose at the heart of the team's work

+ Remove distractions that are hampering performance
+ Keep and maintain meaning in everyday work
+ Pair employees to have them hold each other accountable

+ Nurture radical transparency
+ Take a pause from a heated discussion
+ Resolve a conflict by releasing emotions
+ Prevent conflicts by making trade-offs clear

+ Nurture a culture of candor to have honest, difficult conversations
+ Build psychological safety within the team
+ Address team health with a neutral party

+ Hold more engaging meetings
+ Celebrate holidays across geographies
+ Create bonds among virtual teams, and across different offices
+ Sync up and explore with teammates

+ Create shared memories to solidify the organization's identity
+ Celebrate civic outreach and impact stories
+ Break down silos between teams

+ Achieve closure after a departure
+ Welcome new hires with the company values
+ Create an identity for a temporary team
+ Make orientations engaging

+ Have stability through mergers, acquisitions, and leadership changes
+ Get closure for departments or programs that are closing
+ Manage your org's changing direction

Ritual Index

Chapter 3

Chapter 4

Chapter 5

Conflict & Resilience

Chapter 6

Community

Chapter 7

Change + Transition

Profiles

Nick Hobson   25

Ph.D., Social Psychologist,
University of Toronto

Laura Miner   70

Designer, Founder,
BuddyBuddy Studio

Cipriano Lopez   59

CEO,
Haceb

Ayse Birsel   83

Designer, Artist, Author
Birsel+Seck Studio

Introduction

A Welcome Note

This book offers rituals that can be used to bring new energy and community into your everyday work. Our focus is on bottom-up changes to how we work. Rather than relying on top-down, formal efforts to make work better, rituals can help you create smaller-scale, participatory ways to help people more satisfied, productive, and connected.

Beyond bottom-up rituals, we also present rituals that help your team communicate better. There are also rituals to help organizations make changes and deal with difficulties.

Over the past years, we have taught courses on Ritual Design at Stanford's d.school, with corporate and public service partners, to identify ways to respond to problems around disengagement at work. We began to collect other organizations' and people's rituals to show our students, and to inspire them as they created new rituals for work.

In this book, we showcase a mixture of these rituals—those from well-established companies that have whole teams devoted to culture and community-building, as well as more experimental ones that have emerged from design workshops and sprints. At the end of the book we present the basics of how we run our own ritual design practice. There you'll also find a process to design your own custom rituals.

Throughout the book, we have profiled people who are making new rituals and who are creating better organizational cultures. We feature them, to show examples of how people are experimenting with new ways of working, being creative, and building great relationships.

This book is a practical one, which you can browse and skip through, to find what might be relevant to the challenges you are facing. On page viii-xi, there are 2 overviews of themes and rituals to guide you.

Why Bring Rituals into Work?

We spend so much of our lives at work—whether in a big company, a small startup, or on our own projects. But how much do we invest in making our work lives better, when it comes to our relationships, our creativity, our focus, our life transitions, and the ups-and-downs of our organizations?

Rituals can be one powerful strategy to improve our work lives—and help us act more like we aspire to be. They are practices that can bond people together, help us move through conflicts, amp us up to better performances, and assist us in adapting to change.

Companies and people face big challenges at work today. There are low levels of employee engagement, high levels of stress and fear, inhuman environments, and failed reorganizations.[1] These problems at work require a multi-faceted set of strategies to make more human-centered, values-driven, and creative workplaces. Rituals are one of these strategies, that leaders and individuals can employ to address their big problems.

Sports fans likely are already familiar with rituals for work. Rafael Nadal has an extensive sequence of rituals for his tennis game performance. He takes a cold shower forty-five minutes before every game. This is his work ritual, to regulate his emotions and get into a focused performance and a state of flow.[2]

Zipcar created a ritual to lead their company through a big organizational shift. When they decided to redirect towards a mobile-first company, they brought the company together for a ritual smashing of desktop computers.[3] (See more in Chapter 7.) It was a collective ceremony to mark the end of the old way of working and move to the new.

This book presents the research into why rituals improve work, as well as many more examples to inspire you.

Our goal in this book is to show ways to experiment with more intentional, connected, and meaningful work culture. Using the rituals in this book can be one way to experiment with making your work better.

We know that rituals are not the only solution to tackling the big challenges of work, but they are a distinct and effective strategy to help you put your values, ethics, and goals into practice.

RITUALS
(a definition)

ACTIONS that a PERSON or GROUP does repeatedly, following a similar Pattern or Script, in which they've imbued SYMBOLISM and MEANING.

The Meaning of Ritual

We use the term "ritual" to capture practices that have a special power to make a meaningful moment. They have unique factors that elevate them above normal experiences.

A ritual is an action done following a similar pattern and script, in a particular situation. Most rituals follow a script, with a set path that people will follow and repeat.

They are done with an intent and awareness. Unlike a routine, rituals are not mindless. They are done with people recognizing that something special is happening, that they are tuned into.

They involve some physical movement. There is usually a patterned rhythm of people moving, that activates a sense of something special going on. There are symbols at work. They could be props, words, or actions that represent something bigger—usually a higher value. These symbols invoke a sense of the extraordinary, that transforms the average into the special.

A good ritual tells a story, which often helps a person make sense of something that is going on, figure out what it means in a bigger picture, and deal with it.

They have a je ne sais quoi factor that elevates an average moment into a memorable, charged one. From the outside, a ritual could look irrational or nonfunctional, because it does not always make logical sense.

Rituals at Different Levels

Rituals don't have to be grand or spiritual. They are on a continuum of intensity and frequency.

Some rituals are short and happen often, like daily stand-up meetings in a development team. These may be low intensity, but still carry the benefits of building shared purpose and a sense of community.

Other rituals are dramatic and infrequent, like a graduation ceremony. It has more elaborate scripts, formal actions to take, and a once-in-a-lifetime quality. This can also mean it carries a bigger sense of meaning and connection.

Rituals may seem like a "soft" strategy to make meaningful change, because they do not operate with a direct, transactional logic. But they have value in making abstract organizational identities, goals, and principles concrete. And they produce intangible benefits of shared purpose, a sense of meaning, and community bonds.

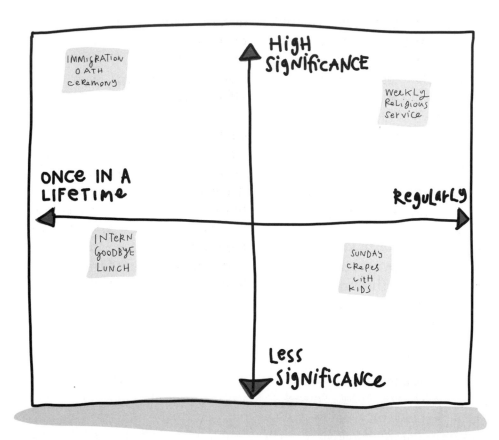

Who Can Use Rituals for Work?

Rituals are about creating meaning: how do we make our lives, our teams, and our products more meaningful? Rituals can help you intentionally create better culture at your work—at the level of a whole organization, a team, or your own practice.

This book is for people who are interested in experimenting with building better work cultures.

It could be a person who wants to make their everyday work routines more productive, more in line with their ethics and goals, or more memorable.

Or it could be a team member or manager who knows their work-life could be more in line with their values, and wants to bring more collaboration, humor, and creativity into their organization.

Or it could be a leader at the helm of an organization who wants to nurture a large-scale culture, that manifests the values and norms of the organization's mission statement, guiding principles, and ethical obligations.

Or it could be a designer or an engineer who is working on an entirely new innovation. They may want to find ways to be more creative, or to roll out the new thing they are making. They may want to experiment with making a culture shift that would help their new innovation succeed.

I want to improve the CULTURE at my organization, to make us stronger & more values-driven.

I am managing a team, and want to build a sense of community, even through many changes and setbacks.

I want to change my own ways of working, to be more creative, focused, & efficient.

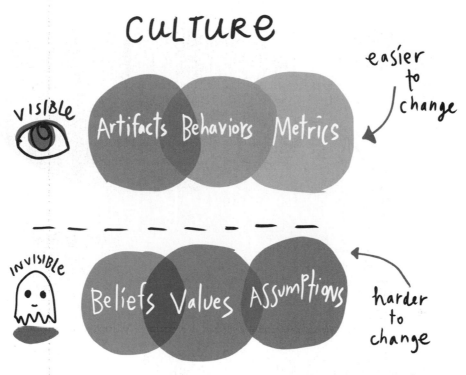

CULTURE

VISIBLE
Artifacts Behaviors Metrics

easier to change

INVISIBLE
Beliefs Values Assumptions

harder to change

Culture Map, adapted from James Heskett's Culture Cycle[4]

In particular, people who are interested in their work community and culture can use rituals. This might be managers or leaders—or even new hires who care about how their organization is run.

Often, the culture of an organization is set by talking in the abstract. This could be through writing down a manifesto, core principles, or a constitution. Rituals are ways to bring these big, abstract ideas into daily practice. By default, they involve physical actions and concrete behaviors. A good ritual will take the underlying values and intangible beliefs of a company—all these valuable, invisible things—and make them visible, interactive, and lively real-world practices throughout the organization.

Can you be an architect of your work life? Even if you are not the manager of your company or your team, you can use lightweight strategies—like rituals—to make work be more like you wish it could be.

This means bringing a sense of practical creativity to work life. What are small experiments and new practices you can try out, to see how you can address the problems you face. It also means being more thoughtful about what powers you have and what type of work you want to do.

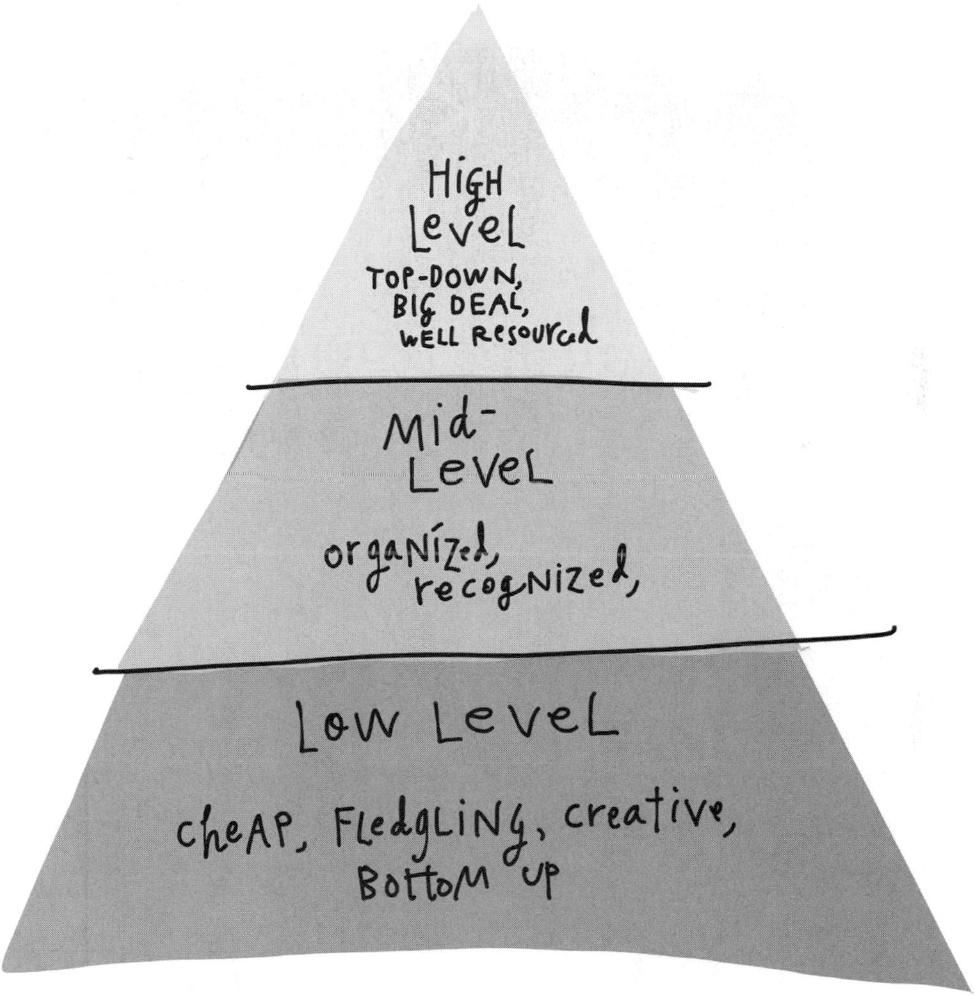

HIGH
LeVeL
TOP-DOWN,
BIG DEAL,
WELL ResourCed

Mid-
LeVeL

orgaNized,
recogNized,

Low LeveL

cheAP, FledgLiNg, creative,
BottoM up

Often, when we think of our WORK CULTURE we think in TOP-DOWN terms: what the leadership does & says, and big, formally-organized events.

What About a
BOTTOM-UP CULTURE,
that is set by
People throughout
an organization—
with RITUALS & other
actions they choose
to do.

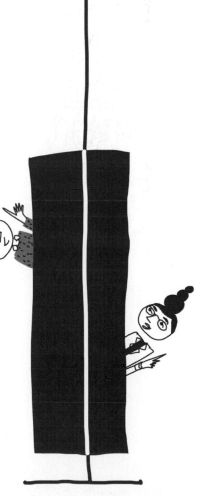

PART ONE

The
Power of
Rituals

1
Rituals for Better Work

The Power of Rituals

Our interest in rituals grew out of our work as designers, as we noticed that some of our most successful projects came when we thought about framing a new product or initiative as a "ritual." Whether it was in promoting adherence to diabetes regimens, helping people prepare for fighting their traffic tickets, or helping new managers oversee their teams more effectively.[5] The frame of ritual worked to make new products more attractive and engaging.[6]

We observed that when we created things using the patterns of a ritual— even if we didn't call our new thing a "ritual"—it became more likely that people would want to use it, and continue to use it. A ritual sets up a clear path for people to follow, and it calls up a sense of meaning and connection—which drew people in.

Rituals have special power to bond people together and to make sense of their world. As we began experimenting with rituals as a means for individual growth and organizational change at work, we learned that in a very short time and with minimal budget, rituals can bring liveliness, lightness, and a sense of community to a group.

Many scholars in anthropology, psychology, neuroscience, and organizational behavior have developed a strong body of research into how rituals work, and what powers they have. This scholarship can help us understand what the origins of rituals are, in evolution and in history. It also describes how rituals operate, and why they matter so much to humans. This research provides empirical support to the many practical, anecdotal examples in this book.

Rituals give order and meaning. Foundational studies of rituals emerged out of the work of sociologist Emile Durkheim. When he studied religion, he discovered rituals as a central backbone to how belief systems operate. Rituals make beliefs concrete and graspable for people.[7] People gravitate toward the function and structured behavior that rituals offer. This structure brings people a sense of things being in their control and with a sense of meaning.

Rituals give people a safe space to experiment.
Anthropologist Clifford Geertz found that when people act out rituals, they can jump from what the "real" world is to another one, that is more ideal.[8] Rituals let people imagine other ways of behaving and living, taking a break from their everyday rules and routines. They give people safe, structured zones to build better ways of living.

MIND

Rituals-
WORK BY
bringing
the 2
ways of
'Processing'
in SyNC

BODY

With more empirical study of rituals, psychologists have discovered that their power derives from their ability to link the physical with the psychological and the emotional—all with the benefit of "regulation."

A recent review of scholarship on rituals found that the actions of physically going through rituals help people feel satisfied and in control.[9] The ritual actions regulate people's emotions, keeping them calm. Rituals also regulate people's performance, helping them to act in a steadier and more focused way. Finally, rituals regulate people's sense of belonging, giving them a stable feeling of social connection.

The Power of Rituals: How and Why They Work

How can we understand if a ritual works, and how it works?

Researchers in social science, business, neuroscience, behavioral science, psychology, and other fields have begun to study rituals' power more empirically. In one track of studies, researchers are measuring the experience and outcomes of rituals through straightforward, objective measurements. On another track, researchers consider more subjective outcomes and experiences, with investigation into people's perceived effectiveness of the rituals, and on physiological changes that result from them.

Increasingly, research teams use controlled trials to measure the power of rituals on various aspects of people's experiences and performance.[10] They gave a treatment group a ritual to perform, and a control group no ritual. Then they measured whether and how the ritual treatment affected the group's performance on a given task, and their psychological and physiological measures.

Rituals increase performance by decreasing anxiety.

Examining pre-performance rituals, Alison Wood Brooks and her colleagues found that rituals increase performance by decreasing the anxiety before a public presentation—a singing contest.[11] The ritual that they created is as follows: Draw a picture of how you are feeling right now. Sprinkle salt on your drawing. Count up to five out loud. Crumple up your paper. Throw your paper in the trash.

They measured the performed ritual's efficacy by asking participants about their emotional state and by measuring their heart rate. They found that rituals decreased anxiety better than both random behaviors and non-rituals. This study suggests that rituals performed before a stressful task can calm their arousal and help them perform better.

Rituals help people deal with negative transitions.

In a study with people who had lost loved ones, researchers Francesca Gino and Michael Norton studied the effects of mourning rituals. They found that rituals reduce people's grief and increase feelings of control in time of uncertainty and loss.[12]

Rituals enhance performance by motivating and bonding people.

To probe the effectiveness of group rituals, Norton and his colleagues created a scavenger hunt that involved taking selfie pictures at specific locations on campus.[13] They asked the ritual group to perform a clapping and foot stomping ritual before the scavenger hunt. The non-ritual group didn't get any such instruction.

At the end, they measured the number of selfies taken. The winner

Harvard researchers found that a made-up ritual like this could decrease people's performance anxiety when they were given a stressful task, like a surprise singing context.

was selected based on the number of group selfies. The ritual group outperformed the non-ritual group. They also reported more cohesion among the team members.

Rituals increase creativity.

The same researchers did another study looking at whether individual or group rituals have a greater effect on creativity.[14] They assigned creative tasks to the study participants, such as brainstorming ways to find uses for a given object. Then they asked them to perform a ritual involving rolling dice and waving their arms in patterns. Some of the participants did this solo, and some others performed it in groups. Results showed that the group ritual increased the participants' creativity and their cohesion better than the solo ritual.

Rituals improve quality of an experience.

Another team of Kathleen Vohs and her colleagues, explored if a ritual could improve people's experiences of eating food. Does a ritual make an experience more valuable?

They asked the experimental group to perform a specific ritual before eating a chocolate.[15] Their instructions: "Without unwrapping the chocolate bar, break it in half. Unwrap half of the bar and eat it. Then, unwrap the other half and eat it." In the no-ritual condition, participants ate the chocolate after they were given some relaxation time. Results showed that performing the pre-eating ritual made the chocolate more flavorful and valuable. The ritual made people savor it more.

Ritual steps and frequency improve its perceived effectiveness.

Other studies have shown that the details of rituals influence how much people perceive them to be effective. In a study conducted in Brazil, researchers Cristine Legare and Andre Souza studied people who perform simpatias: rituals that are used to address chronic issues such as quitting smoking, curing asthma, and warding off bad luck.

People perceived simpatias to be more effective if there were more steps involved. Other factors mattered too, including the repetition of procedures, whether the steps are performed at a specified time, and whether they involved symbols. These all indicate the actions and repetitions of a ritual can have meaningful affect on people's experiences.

Ritual increase feeling of control.

Outside the world of work, rituals can also increase people's ability to make wise choices. Allen Ding Tian and his colleagues looked at rituals' effects on healthy eating habits. They found that performing a ritual increased a person's sense of control in their calorie intake and healthy food choices.[16]

Researchers created a ritual around how to eat a chocolate bar. People found that a pre-eating ritual made the chocolate more flavorful and valuable.

The Principles
of Rituals

PRINCIPLE 1

RITUALS have a Magical, Je-Ne-Sais-QUOI Factor.

PRiNCiPLe
2

RiTUALS Are
DONe with
INTENTIONALiTy
with the person
tuned into this being
a special moment.

PRINCIPLE

3

A RITUAL
carries a
SYMBOLIC
VALUE,
that gives a sense
of purpose & that's
beyond the practical.

PRINCIPLE 4

A RITUAL — EVOLVES OVER TIME to BETTER suit the PEOPLE & the situation.

Five Types of Workplace Rituals

Rituals can serve several purposes at work. We have identified five prominent powers of rituals in organizations. These themes emerged out of our research into organizational rituals and were reaffirmed in our design work.

Creativity and Innovation Rituals

Creativity and innovation fuel an organization. To keep up with changing markets and performance, an organization needs to be creative across its operations and teams. Creativity rituals' spark can help people find inspiration and build off of each others' ideas. Artists, writers, and filmmakers use the structure and repetition of rituals to achieve creativity.[17]

Design teams use creativity rituals to build a generative environment, where people move past anxieties about 'getting it right' and brainstorming new ideas. These rituals can also build empathetic connections that inspire innovation, by building bonds with people outside one's normal circles.

Performance and Flow Rituals

As research suggests, rituals help individuals and teams boost confidence and focus prior to taking on a challenge. These can be before high-stakes things like a board meeting, or it can be around the small challenges of creative daily work. Performance rituals tap into the beliefs and props that individuals already value, and use them to inspire better work.

Many athletes use rituals to improve their performance, whether it's doing particular sequences of warm-up movements, eating the same special combination of food, hitting a teammate in their pads, kissing an old jersey, or putting gum on a trampled part of the field.[18]

Conflict and Resilience Rituals

Work life can take a different turn when egos clash, projects fail, or political maneuvers heat up people's temper. In those times, there are many paths to take, including avoidance, mitigation, and burning bridges Conflict and resilience rituals can help people deal with difficult times.

For example, Native Americans' smudging ceremonies take place after there's been a high-stakes clash between two groups.[19] After a conflict has flared up, then the groups follow a symbolic act of enjoying the company through smudging. The ritual cleanses negative emotions and resets the tone between the two.

Community and Team Building Rituals

We are wired to create rituals to bond with one another and build communities. When we perform community rituals, we grow a strong sense of belonging and identity. Our collective beliefs get acted out and they are reinforced in the group.

We see community rituals woven through our lives. There are elaborate college sports tailgating rituals, with special food and music. Festivals like Burning Man use costumes and the burning of a wooden temple to construct fledgling communities. Religious communities bond with ceremonies and meals.

The rituals help the group to express what matters to them, and to explore the identity of the group. It helps people in the group feel like they belong with each other, and share something profound.

Org Change and Transition Rituals
We have life cycles in our work, like
we do in our personal life. As an
organization grows, new employees
join, projects kick off, and teams
form. Fast forward months and
years: some people leave, projects
get completed, and teams dissolve.
And sometimes an organization
dramatically changes its direction
with lay-offs, reorganizations, and
leadership changes.

Whether it's during growth or
decline, these periods can be very
unsettling. Transition rituals can
help people mark these changes and
overcome the tensions around uncertainty—much like personal rituals
to mark transitions of graduation,
marriage, death, and birth.[20] Onboarding new members, saying goodbye
to departing people, shutting down
projects, and reorganizing teams
are transition moments where rituals
can be meaningful.

2

How to Bring Rituals into Your Work, Team, and Org

You may have a hunch that rituals could make a difference in your work life—that you could have better ways of working day to day, or that you could improve how your team functions, or inspire a better sense of community.

As you think about which specific ritual might work best for your situation, there are some key mindsets to adopt—those of a anthropologist, and those of a designer.

Anthropologist

Adopt an open mind when you look at your own work life and your organization. Be a keen observer of the situations as they exist. Spot where there are sparks of "meaning" that already occur. Tune into when people are talking about their values, beliefs, and goals. And articulate people's everyday routines and aspirations.

Designer

"Everyone designs who devises courses of action aimed at changing existing situations into preferred ones," writes Herbert Simon, the Nobel Laureate, in *The Sciences of the Artificial*.[21] Embrace the designer role, by trying new experiments to see what works—and by using your existing materials, like routines, spaces, and goals.

We have identified several strategies to help you in deploying rituals.

1. Create a safe space.
To bring rituals into a group, the most important thing is openness and transparency among partici-pants. To achieve this, create the means for a space where members can explore the core values and issues together and design a ritual accordingly.

2. Facilitate ritual design.
To make your ritual successful, you need alignment and collective buy-in from your team members. Use design methods to facilitate conver-sations, and create alignment.

3. Seed advocates.
In every endeavor, you will have more interest from some who believe in the need and value of a ritual more than the others. Find those people and seed them inside a group. They can also be the facilita-tors of the ritual.

4. Don't impose a top-down ritual.
For a new ritual to take off, there's no way to command people to participate without sparking a back-lash—and defeating the purpose of it. Instead, set a context for people to do the ritual in their own way, so they are supported with a structure but are allowed to decide exactly what it is and how to do it.

5. Don't call it a ritual.
Particularly if you're trying to convince your colleagues who may be skeptical of culture-building exercises, you can simply do the new thing, or ask for them to humor you—without putting a formal label of what this thing is, or that it is a ritual.

6. Keep it cheap and lightweight.
You can create rituals without requesting a huge budget, arranging large time obligations, or putting too much effort into complicated arrangements. When first rolling out a ritual, keep it scrappy to see if it sticks. Run short test runs, to see if it's a good fit.

7. Tap into the charisma of an instigator.

Getting a ritual off the ground, it takes a willingness to suspend analytical thinking. Who in your organization has the ability to bring out others' creativity and playfulness? They should be involved in the launch. Find "early adopters," who are already keyed into doing things differently, and empower them to be leaders in the culture.

8. Don't mix it up with routine.

Rituals can have routine qualities, but rituals are not routines. A ritual is an intentional act; it needs you to be present and committed when it's happening. Routines, on the other hand, are automated, and often only get recognized when they're broken.

9. Rituals can be a means to build up habits.

That being said, building a habit is not building a ritual. Rituals carry a core of meaning and values, which can help an individual or group to get motivated or regulate their emotions in the way to build a habit.

10. Get beyond the "fun."

Not all rituals are positive. When designing for people and teams, we suggest that our participants go beyond just the most obvious rituals—which tend to be around creating 'fun' energy and structuring the day. That means looking for low points in our working lives. For instance, for a manager, we designed a ritual for a conflict, to mitigate and increase the resilience of the team members.

11. Make the rituals here your own.

The book is full of examples, but don't use them as strict recipes. Adapt them to your own work culture by drawing from your own history, values, in-jokes, routines, and symbols. These rituals can be inspiration, but you'll need to customize them intentionally to see if they work for you.

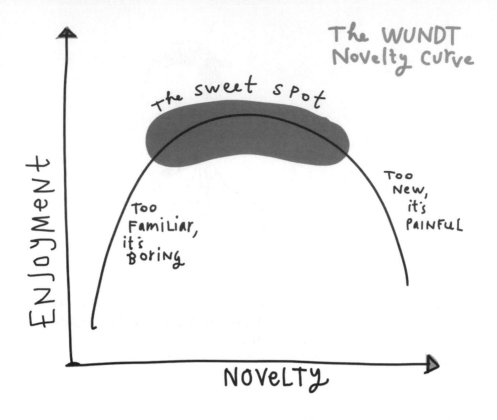

The WUNDT Novelty Curve

the sweet spot

ENJOYMENT

Too Familiar, it's Boring

Too New, it's Painful

NOVELTY

12. Know they don't always live forever. Rituals are not always meant to permanent institutions. We know from our workshops that many expire once they lose their meaning, or as the organization shifts. That's okay—keep them for as long as they are useful, and then move on if they aren't sticking. Don't force a ritual.

13. Don't overwhelm people at first. Following the Wundt novelty curve,[22] you have to introduce a ritual in "the sweet spot,"—where the experience feels new, but not too new. Thanks to Isabel Behncke for telling us about it. If a new ritual is loaded with novelty—something that requires people to behave radically different than they normally do, or that puts them in a very strange context— they'll disengage out of pain. But if it's not different enough than the status quo, people will disengage out of boredom. A ritual can be a growing thing—start low-key, and then gradually more elements can be layered on.

Nick Hobson

Social Psychologist, Neuroscientist
University of Toronto

Work on Rituals

Nick's work examines the psychology and neuroscience of rituals. He began studying rituals in 2011 at the start of his PhD.

At that time, there was not a single empirical psychology paper on rituals. He wondered: how was it that a field claiming to understand the fundamentals of human behavior had so little to say about one of the most pervasive and culturally ubiquitous behaviors known to humans? And how was it that in all the century of ritual scholarship, we didn't have a science of ritual?

Clearly it was an area ripe for research. So, he decided to dedicate his graduate training to advancing the psychology (and science) of ritual. He began to analyze existing rituals—especially collective ones—to understand how they work. Nick started researching how rituals operate in groups, to bind them together, but also to possibly "blind" them with biases. He then began to study more psychological and neurological outcomes that rituals have, both at the personal level and collective one.

Nick's Rituals at Work

It's funny, when Nick started studying rituals, he made up his mind that he would never engage in rituals himself.

Having the mindset of a hyper-rational scientist, he came to see rituals as too irrational for his tastes. His opinion has changed over the years. After all, as scholars have long noted, just because rituals appear to have no direct function, doesn't necessarily mean they are pointless. Quite the opposite. In fact, it's precisely because of ritual's irrationality that they are such an important part of life. His personal experiences align with the research findings: the more rituals, the better.

This is also true in Nick's world of work. So for him, he tries to build mini-rituals as a way to organize his team members around the company's culture and values. His team is a purely remote team, which presents the challenge of adopting rituals that are digitally enacted.

He says, "You have to be creative. One of these we refer to as the Virtual Watercooler. We carve out a set amount of time each week to just shoot the breeze. Two rules apply: One, you have to have a favorite drink in your hand. And two, the topic you choose to chat about can't be related to work."

Another ritual for him, personally, is for whenever he works from home. He has to organize his surroundings "just so" before he launches into the day's tasks. On the window sill in front of him sits only two things. On the right, there's a phrenology head statue slightly angled to face him. And on the left, a diffuser that energizes his senses with a peppermint mist. He says, "Silly, I know. But it works. Plus, the science confirms: placebos are capable of altering brain states."

Suggestions to Others Who Want to Work for Better Culture

Nick recommends that people have more rituals, though it's easier said done. From anthropological and historical research, Nick knows that the strongest cultures and communities were deeply ritualistic. Rituals were

the reason for their success. They helped quell collective angst, they helped provide discipline, but above all, they galvanized people around a common cause. This idea, called "identity fusion," is what happens when a group goes from being just a bunch of individuals to a collection that is far more than the sum of its parts. It's the Durkheimian ethic of collective effervescence in which the individual self-transcends and moves from the plane of the profane to the sacred.

So, Nick asks: Can this complicated concept be applied to the modern world of work? Can we strive for identity fusion and sacredness in our high-tech organizations? Probably not to the same extent that we see it in religions, he finds. But perhaps that's only because religions have been around for millennia versus the single decade lifespan of most companies.

But at any rate, Nick finds that the best rituals are ones that are formed spontaneously and have time to take a more formal shape. The opposite will likely fail. So a manager, for example, who's mandating that her team do a particular ritual for the betterment of the group, will not see that ritual succeed. If anything, it will backfire. Rituals are organic products that happen when people come together and rally around a shared goal or identity.

So instead, the goal of that manager should be to allow the ritual (any ritual) to happen and form on its own. As she begins to notice one taking shape, her job is to simply make sure that the ritual becomes ... well, ritualized.

Excitement for the Future of Work

The excitement that Nick has for the future of work is more of a nervous excitement. His apprehension is due to a shift in the conventional norms of how we work. As we become more technologically advanced, Nick sees that rituals will become a relic of the "old work." These days, the focus is on digital disruption for the purposes of maximizing efficiencies of the process. The problem is, rituals are rife with inefficiencies.

It's possible, then, that we'll see fewer rituals being done in organizations as an attempt to make employees more productive and less costly. Nick sees no merit in this view: a community (at work or otherwise) that lacks rituals lacks lasting success. So thinking about return on investment and a company's bottom line, there's a definite return on rituals.

PART TWO

50 Rituals for Work

3
Creativity and Innovation Rituals

Creativity and innovation happen when people break the script and make non-obvious connections. Rituals can provide a structure for people to switch to a creative mindset and push the boundaries of the ordinary. They can also help teams develop a culture of experimentation.

When Would You Use a Creativity Ritual?

Individual
+ Fire up the right brain
+ Bring dead projects to life
+ Start building things quickly

Team
+ Encourage lateral thinking
+ Giving license to risk and fail
+ Inspire the team with idea building
+ Meet people where they are struggling

Organization
+ Develop solutions for recurring issues
+ Create a culture of ideation and controlled risk-taking
+ Encourage everyone to share their skills

10 Creativity and Innovation Rituals

1 The Daily Drawing
Fire Up the Right Brain Before Creative Work

2 The Zombie Garden
Bring Back Dead Projects to Life

3 The Idea Party
Celebrate and Encourage a Culture of Ideation

4 The Fixathon
Spark Solutions for Recurring Issues In your Organization

5 Design Mad Libs
When You Need to Stretch Your Team's Imagination

The DaiLy DRAWING
Fire up the Right Brain Before your creative work

1. The Daily Drawing

 The Use Case

When you need to fire up your right brain right before creative work or any kind of serious work.

 Org Ritual

This is best done solo, to take all the pressure off doing "work"—though team members can do it in parallel.

 Props

+ Paper
+ Pen
+ Any kind of reminder.

 Difficulty Level

It's an easy ritual; however, props and affordances need to be placed well, like a white paper and pen in front of you every morning.

What is the ritual?

Once a person sits down at their desk, they take out a card or a notebook sheet, and then spend exactly one minute doodling anything they like. It can be something they will work on, something they are thinking about, or a random sketch. The only rule is that it must be a drawing and it must take one minute—not more, not less.

Rather than start the day at the desk with the computer and emails, this ritual starts the day with a small creative challenge. If it's done every day, it becomes a low-barrier activity to jumpstart creativity without too much thinking or planning.

How It Works

The goal of the Daily Drawing is to be loose and easy with creative work. The rules of the ritual mean that you have to draw something, and you have to do is quickly. It doesn't have to be good, it just has to happen. This structure should reduce the pressure on quality, and should make it easier to get started on creative work.

The person can choose what they do with the doodle. It may go up on a growing board, to make a progressive sequence of drawings. Or it can be tucked into a notebook, put into a drawer, shared with someone else, or even ripped up. The drawing doesn't have to be useful beyond just waking up your creativity.

How to Adapt

Often we start our classes at the Stanford d.school with the Daily Drawing ritual. Each person does their own sketch on a index card, and then everyone posts their drawings together on a whiteboard. This is meant to get the whole team to be creative, and to reset everyone from whatever other class or activity they are coming from, into a design mindset.

Another type of Daily Drawing is the "center page" drawing, intended for a person setting their agenda for the day. Designer Ayse Birsel does this to start her focus and work every morning. This helps offset the intimidation she feels at the start of every day and the blank page—starting again from scratch. Then she writes the one central thing she wants to think about or work on at the center of the blank page. From there she doodles, mindmaps, and writes all around it. But the page helps her think through what is going on and what she can do with the rest of her day.

The Crack of Dawn Variation

One variation of the Daily Drawing is the "Crack of Dawn" drawing. This comes from Ayse Birsel, and her morning practices.

Even if you are not a morning person—especially if you are not a morning person—you can hold a creative session for yourself before you have fully woken up.

Set your clock for 2 hours earlier than you normally would. Have a small treat planned for yourself—coffee, tea, biscuit, what you like. Take the treat and go to your creative space, whether it is writing or drawing.

Before your brain starts warming up—and before your ego kicks in to make you feel anxious or self critical—get to your creative work with drawings—or writing and more. The point of the Morning Drawing is to ramp up the day with a small, meditative, creative action. It can relieve the stress and can set the "flow."

IN YOUR TEAM,
ANY IDEA that DOESN'T
MOVE FORWARD gets
WRITTEN ON A CARD &
PINNED To THE
GraveYARD WALL.

IF YOU WANT to
BRING the PROJECT
BACK To LIFE,
MOVE that CARD
over to the
ZomBie GARDEN.

ONCe you get it
to ImPLeMENTation,
ADD a NEW PLANT
to the GardeN, bury
the card in it +
Name the PLANT after
the project.

The ZOMBIE GARDEN

Bring DEAD PROJects Back to LIFe

2. The Zombie Garden

 The Use Case

When you need to rescue (or kill) half-dead projects in your organization, because the baggage is hampering people's motivation.

 Org Ritual

Org ritual—and teams can do the same ritual for their projects.

 Props

+ A wall or canvas
+ Cards
+ Plants

 Difficulty Level

This is a medium-level ritual, which requires the dedication of a particular space and facilitation to tend the garden and projects.

What Is the Ritual?

The Zombie Garden is a ritual for when there are too many half-alive projects that are burdening an organization. This ritual makes these zombie projects visible on a Graveyard Wall, and challenges people to take action on them. If they revive them, and bring them to resolution, then they join a garden. Otherwise, if they continue to languish without anyone claiming them, then they are officially killed and everyone must move on.

The Zombie Garden is a way to recognize old projects and bring back to life those that people want to work on. It makes these somewhat painful projects visible, as candidates for reincarnation. And it can help make an organization more clearly decisive about where it will spend its limited resources.

How It Works

Organizational life is full of half-dead projects. Priorities change as teams shrink or expand, and the market pulls or pushes. Hackathons create huge amounts of new half-baked projects. When projects stall out, people often have a bad taste—because their work is not paying off and progress is not being made.

An organization can make a Zombie Garden to deal with these kinds of semi-abandoned and half-dead projects. The Zombie Garden helps an organization to recognize the work that's been done, even it isn't fully made. It can bring closure for failed projects. And it helps teams that are looking to leverage past projects with potential, helping them scout new work.

- A wall is designated as the Project Graveyard, and anyone can post a project that they think is a zombie—mostly dead, not resolved, but with the possibility of revival.

- Next to the wall is a garden of pots with small clips stuck in them. If anyone wants to claim a Zombie project, they take the card from the Graveyard wall, sign it, and clip it in a planter.

- If they get the project to resolution, then they get a plant. The card is torn up and scattered into the plant's dirt, and the plant stays in the garden. It is named after the project

- Any project card that is not claimed in a month is now officially "dead" and it is removed from the wall.

The Idea Party

Celebrate and encourage a culture of ideation

3. The Idea Party

 The Use Case

When you want to celebrate a team's creative spirit, and also get more people's input on what should move forward.

 Org Ritual

Everyone in an organization should be invited to the party, and the team members can be the "hosts" to present their work.

 Props

+ Foam boards or an empty wall with visuals
+ Voting dots or ballots for selection process

 Difficulty Level

This is a medium-cost, medium-planning ritual. Some initial prep is needed to organize the event and the visuals.

What Is the Ritual?

An Idea Party is a way to celebrate the end of a workshop or other hands-on session, and to loop the rest of your organization into the creative work through a lightweight event. The Idea Party is an event that should happen right after a creative session, in which the work product from the session is laid out like a gallery. Ideas and insights are displayed on big foam boards or walls. Others are invited to mingle and tour around with drinks and snacks. They can ask questions, leave comments, and then rank which should move forward.

This ritual is meant to recognize the hard work of the team, and then build on others' expertise to refine their creative work before moving forward.

How It Works

Have you ever been through a very thorough and engaging project workshop—but you've struggled to have the rest of the organization appreciate the work? The Idea Party is an alternative to slide presentations, reports, or email summaries about creative work. It's a cross of a cocktail party, a museum experience, and a pitch competition.

- Once a creative session concludes, each team is responsible for making their work into a poster to include in the gallery.

- The whole organization (and outsiders too) are invited for an hour of snacks, drinks, and interesting ideas.

- The facilitator kicks off the party with a salute to the team's hard work, and the goals of the session.

- Then the facilitator announces the surprise: the poster with the most votes gets a special prize.

- Let everyone mingle easily—and then with ten minutes left, announce that votes must be submitted.

- Count the votes, and the team with the highest votes gets a prize—a basket of gifts, funding for the project, or something else.

- Make sure posters live longer than the party to increase exposure and impact. They can be hung in the halls, until the next Idea Party.

How to Adapt

Some companies do a similar activity, with concept posters. For example, Amazon has teams create a "Cover Story at the Start," in which ideas at early stages are made into front-page magazine covers. This is to help build excitement and clarity around rough ideas. An Idea Party's posters might be done as magazine covers like this.

Flipboard, a Palo Alto technology company, holds Mock O'Clock. It's a regular shareout of prototypes and concepts, like a show-and-tell for what's being developed. This is a way to share ideas in a low-key and interactive way. A Mock O'Clock doesn't require the budget of a party, and it makes the social sharing of ideas more of regular occurrence in a company.

The Idea Party ritual can also be adapted into meetings where people are tired of sitting through slide presentations. Instead of holding a slide pre-sentation around a boardroom table, have all presenters create foam board stations. Then participants can tour around the ideas, talk them through, and take them in at their own pace. This makes for a more immersive and social sharing of ideas—and hopefully prevents people from tuning out from good ideas because they're burnt out from sitting through slide presentations.

The FixathoN
Spark solutions for recurring issues in your organization

4. The Fixathon

 The Use Case

When there is a recurring problem with a product or service offering that needs attention.

 Org Ritual

Everyone in an organization should be invited to the event, and attendance should be required.

 Props

+ Pen
+ Paper
+ Stickies
+ Food

+ Event
+ Awards—if
  any

Difficulty Level

This is a medium-cost and medium planning ritual—it needs coordination between teams and sponsorship for the food and logistics.

What Is the Ritual?

When an organization has been talking around a problem for a long time, a Fixathon is a ritual event to force people to focus on getting this problem solved. It takes the intensity of a hackathon—work in a concentrated sprint—and directs it to a specific innovation that needs to happen.

In a Fixathon, a whole organization comes together and works until the problem is addressed. People from across functions work together, and everyone is focused on the same task at once—to remove the usual barriers of logistics, space, and silos that slow work down.

The event is run strictly around time. This builds pressure and dedication among everyone to get the problem solved.

How It Works

The Fixathon is like an Amish barn-raising ritual—the whole community comes together to work in sync, and quickly achieve a huge task that otherwise would take months.

- Choose a clear, necessary problem to be solved at the Fixathon. The organizers can poll people beforehand about what problem or innovation to focus on. If the organization is large, a handful of goals are set. For example, a Fixathon could be about helping an under-performing product team, addressing a recurring complaint from customers, or giving pro-bono help to a non-profit.

- Everyone in the organization is informed of the date, the timing, and the purpose of the Fixathon. They can prep beforehand, to make sure that they know the challenges and what skills they can bring to solving it. Everyone in the organization has to clear their schedules—the Fixathon is mandatory and should be the sole priority of everyone.

- On the day of the Fixathon, the facilitator can help form teams and introduce people who don't normally work together. They will also set the timer, and keep all the teams on track—with checkpoints, share-outs, and planning on how to get the tasks done in the remaining time.

- The event should have lots of food, drinks, and space to spread out. There can be breaks to exercise, play games, and review others' work. People are allowed to leave, but the facilitators should encourage everyone to be fully present and on topic.

- As the Fixathon nears the end, the facilitators should start a countdown, to build the event to a climax.

- At the end, all the teams share what they've done. Ideally, there is a celebration to commemorate that the problem has been solved.

How to Adapt

The same methods of a Fixathon can be used for more divergent purposes—to have people throughout an organization develop new, different ideas in a concentrated way.

Facebook regularly runs Hackathons, in which teams have 24 hours to work on something they don't normally work on day-to-day. Anyone, from an intern to a senior employee can form a team to create something new. Teams present to executives, showing off their prototypes for the chance to get their development put into the main pipeline of projects.

Flipboard organizes an annual event called the Mockathon.[23] It's part of their internship program. In this case, each of the teams can choose a project to work on in a concentrated way. It's less about fixing a large company-wide problem, and more about working on something important in small teams.

The event is one of the last things Flipboard interns do before going back to school—and it's meant to be a big, memorable experience. Everyone can choose team names, create a mantra, and bond together in their groups as they work crazy hours to develop new things together. In their case, people camp out with sleeping bags and tents, working for almost 24 hours and not leaving the office. Facilitators patrol the teams with megaphones reminding them of the countdown, and encouraging their progress. At the end, there are 2-minute share-outs—and the winning teams get money and awards.

DESIGN MAD LIBS
When you NEED to stretch
your team's imagination

5. Design Mad Libs

The Use Case

When the team is in the trenches of routine work, and needs to switch modes to creative work.

Team Ritual

This is a team ritual, and can become an organizational ritual.

Props

+ Pen
+ Paper
+ Stickies

Difficulty Level

This is a low-cost and low-planning ritual—it just takes the team's buy-in to make sure it happens.

What Is the Ritual?

Design Mad Libs is a quick ritual game in which teams are challenged to imagine and build absurd things. The team comes together and is given a frame—a Mad Lib, with missing words—that they fill in with random words that they draw from a stack of cards or a hat.

It becomes a nonsensical design challenge to create a new physical or digital thing. The team must work together to build, draw, or act out this new thing. They have 4 minutes to make something. Then they start over with a new set of words to create a new prompt, and to make this new thing.

How It Works

Many people already played Mad Libs games as kids, so it is easy to adapt to a design atmosphere. The goal here is to get the team creating and imagining things together—in a safe, absurdist way so that team members are less precious or anxious about their ideas.

- Have a facilitator introduce the rules and keep the groups moving forward rapidly. They can hand out the Mad Libs template, and then get the teams working through this basic schedule.

- Pick cards for the first round, and lay them out into the template.

- Brainstorm ideas and note them down on a sketch.

- Repeat the process through the fourth round. After the fourth round do a share-out.

The concepts that are created during Mad Libs can feed into the project's vision or ideation sessions. It can also be done purely for humor and playfulness. The facilitator can set a rule for what the "output" should be: sketches, storyboards, or skits. These ideas then can be displayed in teams' space to initiate further conversations, and to be a touchstone for this type of creative, playful work.

The team can also deliberately select the prompts—choosing ones that are linked to the domain that they are working on. For instance, MIT Media Lab has a platform of prompts for design work—with words to use for artifacts, inspiration, experience, attributes and medium.[24] The Ritual Design Lab, our project, has an app IdeaPop that has a library full of prompts for workplace experience design, with phrases, contexts, and props to inspire new ritual designs.[25]

Especially if you want to use this ritual to spark new ideas for a project, then it's worth spending time to curate the prompts that the teams will be mixing up and working with.

The FAILURE WAKE PARTY

Celebrate failure to give license to take creative risks

6. The Failure Wake Party

 The Use Case

When the team has failed after an experiment.

 Org Ritual

This is an organizational ritual, that can be scaled back to a team or cross-function teams.

 Props

+ Visualize the project and its steps with a poster
+ Prepare desserts to lighten the mood

 Difficulty Level

This is a medium-level ritual. Organizers will have to arrange a space, food, drink, and light presentations from the team.

What Is the Ritual?

The Failure Wake Party is to celebrate the failure of an experiment. It should encourage the team to take risks and to have a closure. Team members get together around food and music. Leaders can say a few words about what's happened, thank all the team members, and remind them that it's okay to fail—that they're encouraged to experiment. This ritual has been used by a pharmaceutical company to keep employees engaged and motivated in an environment where a high-percentage of failure is normal.[26]

It is set up like a wake, a party after a death, with food, music, and community. Team members can use this event to process what's happened, and the leadership can use it to reinforce core values of the organization.

How It Works

The Failure Wake Party happens when a project has failed in a major way. This could be when a new code change takes down an entire website. Or when a company experiment fails to show promising results, and has to be shut down. Sometimes it can be a correctable mistake, or it can be one that fully ends a years-long endeavor.

- The Failure Wake Party should be set up as an in-person event that is respectful but still joyful. All the team members who contributed to the project are invited, and they can be given a chance to speak if they like.

- A team leader should prepare remarks like a eulogy, recognizing the life cycle of the project and expressing appreciation for everyone's hard work.

- The leader should also signal in their remarks that, despite the failure, the team members should keep working on risky, ambitious experiments—that this failure is not shameful, and should not discourage more innovation work.

The pharmaceutical company Roche throws champagne lunch parties for their teams after a promising compound fails in testing.[27] Their goal is to sustain teams' creativity and dedication to innovation, even when failures happen. The celebration helps people get a sense of closure for a project, and give leadership a chance to show support and appreciation. Ideally, the Failure Wake Party will keep employees engaged, even while working in an industry with a high rate of failed projects.

The Failure Wake Party can be adapted to quicker failure celebrations. For example, if a small failure happens, the team can have a failure celebration moment—to cheer, to eat a special candy, or to pass around a gift—that reaffirms to employees that it is okay to fail if they do so when experimenting on making things better.

The Surprise RIDE ALONG
Get out of the office + connect with
your people for a flash of empathy

7. The Surprise Ride Along

The Use Case

When you need to charge leaders with more empathy with the users, and find sparks for innovation.

Org Ritual

This is an organizational ritual, can be scaled back to a team or cross-function teams.

Props

+ Travel route
+ Messaging app

Difficulty Level

This is a high-cost and high-planning ritual, that takes coordination and a budget to arrange.

What is the ritual?

The Surprise Ride Along is a way to disrupt a project, with leaders whisked away from offices and boardrooms and into the field. They are challenged to set aside their preconceived plans and spend the day listening, watching, and observing the people the project is meant to benefit. It's a ritual that's about radical empathy and finding new paths for creativity.

The organizers should arrange the Ride Along like a surprise party—the team members shouldn't know it's coming, and they should think that they'll be going about work as usual. Then they'll be told that they're actually going to be spending the day shadowing a customer or serving as front-line staff.

The Ride Along has both a symbolic and functional purpose. The act of spending the day listening and observing should reinforce the value of empathy. And the face-to-face experience can catalyze better work by focusing leaders on specific problems and empathetic understanding of others' experiences.

How It Works
The Ride Along demands a high degree of planning, just like a surprise party. The facilitator needs to arrange a decoy event for team members to attend, and then surprise them on the day with a pre-planned field trip. This can be with a pre-selected worker or customer, or it can be in playing the role of a worker or customer in a specific setting.

The team members should not be told too much of where they are going, and they also shouldn't be given a specific "task" to accomplish during their Ride Along. The point is to be surprised, to go with whatever happens, and to take in all of the details in order to make sense of them later. It's a guerrilla event, that should be unstructured. Team members will have to adjust to the field context rather than the other way around.

The Ride Along should end with a thank you to all the people who were shadowed, with small gifts for them to show appreciation for opening their lives to the team. The team can then do a debrief on their way back to the office—drawing sketches, writing down insights, and preserving the spirit of the day to fuel future work.

How to Adapt

There are many different versions of this ritual. In one instance, a CEO of a company flew his executive team with his private jet to meet a customer who was struggling with their company's service. The executives had to speak and work directly with this customer, to see the service from her perspective and interact directly with her (rather than talk about general customers in the abstract.)

In another instance, the CEO of Latin American company Haceb (profiled on the next page) made it mandatory for the executive team to ride with the truck drivers in the company and experience their struggles firsthand. This was to give leaders a view from a completely different perspective.

At Zappos, a version of the Ride Along is part of all new employees' training. When new people start at the company, they spend the first weeks on the front lines of customer service, answering calls from customers. This gives all new employees a strong empathetic experience, to see what customers need and want. No matter what job they are going to, they need to be directly in touch with the customer and their coworkers.

Ride Alongs might already happen in a company—with designers and researchers in a team going out in the field with an empathetic mindset. This surprise ritual gets people from throughout the organization to understand how each other works, and how their work is impacting customers and users. It can reinforce people's sense of purpose and can inspire new directions for innovation.

Cipriano Lopez
CEO, Haceb

Work on rituals
Cipriano is the CEO of HACEB, a Colombian household appliances company. He has used ritual trips to help his team better understand their customers' lives and contexts—and to stay user-focused In their work.

The idea came to him after a tough year in sales, and he began to visit stores in person to see the customers himself. His first response was to develop a discipline to address issues in a faster manner, and to make the customers in the middle of the process and not at the end. However, this wasn't getting translated to the broader team—things didn't change. This made him realize that he needed a strategy to connect executives, field operations, and end users.

So he experimented with the format of his executive team meetings. Cipriano and his team replaced their quarterly meeting with a special road trip. Now instead of spending time together in a conference room, he and his entire management team hit the road, drive to cities, and meet both the field employees and customers to connect to their reality. He says that before these trips the work culture wouldn't change, but once they began to travel together to the field, it was magic.

Cipriano and his colleagues organized these trips in an agile manner. Everything is coordinated through a WhatsApp group. They wake up at 5 am in the morning, sometimes drive to five to six small towns to do visits, and to talk to customers and salespeople. They eat the local food and get to socialize. Cipriano mentions that it's critical to make it fun and engaging. When the field employees see the entire executive team in front of their door, it changes their perception of the culture—breaking down the usual bubbles that keep employees separated.

Impact and Learning

The field trips impacted the misperceptions among internal departments. The assumptions that salespeople and management had about each other—like that management didn't want to get their hands dirty—changed when the executives went into the field, drove with them on their job, helped them carry fridges, and fixed things together. Cipriano observed this practice lowered barriers, to flatten the hierarchy and reinforce that everyone has the same objective.

Based on one of these trips, the company also discovered a new service to be offering. On a field visit, his team realized it's so hard to find parts for some of the products, and the wait time was unbearable. Now they are going to fix this through a new program that offers more immediate tooling services.

The company is also now extending the trip practice, into the onboarding of new managers. Managers start their job with fieldwork where they ride on delivery trucks and meet customers. They also make visits to their own employees' homes and make connections with their reality.

Working for Better Communities and Culture

Cipriano recommends that the Ride Along ritual is replicable, but it has to be authentic. For instance, when he started Ride Along, it came from his love for travel. He used to backpack, and talk to people on his trips—it became part of him. But not everyone can do it. For that reason, you have to prepare your team. The leader of the practice must help the team adapt to it, and tap into their own motivations. It's fun to get away from emails, meetings, smartphones. It's good to get a fresh perspective.

One key thing is to run the trip in a small safe group, but one that has a diversity of backgrounds and demographics. The people have to feel like they are working and they are traveling, but also having fun. Also be prepared to listen to the teams you visit. Often during the visits, the salespeople and frontline staff will be happy for the visit, and they will share with honesty what they like and don't like about the company. This means that executives should be prepared for responsibilities and making commitments that they'll have to fulfill later. It's worth planning for having creative interactions in the field.

Each company needs to build their own way of running a ritual, Cipriano says. There are some basic ideas to borrow, and then you have to figure out the pain points and measures that work for you. It's also very important to have humility mixed with good processes—to give up control while still creating structures that let people take risks, be flexible, and discover creative opportunities.

The Surrealist Portraits
Inspire your Team with a ROUND-ROBIN COLLABORATION

8. The Surrealist Portraits

 The Use Case

At the start of a creative session, when you need to inspire the team work and idea building.

 Team Ritual

This is a team ritual to open meetings or workshops with.

 Props

+ Paper
+ Pen
+ Timer

 Difficulty Level

This is a low-cost and low-planning ritual—just paper, pens, and ten minutes at the start of a meeting.

What Is the Ritual?

The Surrealist Portraits is a round robin ritual for a team that's about to do creative work together. It is drawn from a parlor game played by the Surrealists, called Exquisite Corpse, in which artists would pass around half-done phrases and pictures for others to gradually build from and complete.

In this ritual game, each person starts with a piece of blank paper, and they draw parts of their team-members' portrait before passing it other team members to complete. One person starts with the hair, a second adds the eyes, then a third the nose and lips, and the fourth the chin and shoulders.

The goal is to get the team collaborating on a creative project in a short and funny way, to create something personal for one other, and to begin figuring out how to combine their styles and pay closer attention to other team members.

How It Works

Get a creative meeting going by starting off with a portrait session—done with a quick collaboration around the group.

- Each person takes a piece of paper, folds it into fourths, and writes their name on top of it.

- They pass it around, and one person at a time fills in one-fourth of their portrait.

- One person draws the top quarter of their portrait, then the next person draws the second quarter, and so on—until each person has a finished portrait.

- The final portraits get scanned in, and can be made into a collage group portrait to make into a poster or swag.

How to Adapt

There are other adaptations of group portrait exercises. If you are in a big group of people who don't know one other well, and you want to bring them together to brainstorm—you can have them each start a drawing. Then after about 20 seconds, call "Switch," and have them hand their drawing to another person. The new person can continue the drawing for another 30 seconds, until you call "Switch," and a third person finishes the drawing. This helps create a playful, loose environment where people begin to trust one another.

There's also another version that is geared toward selfless creativity. In this version, everyone in the group folds their paper into three. In the first round, team members create an idea and pass it to the next person. The second person looks at the idea and writes down on the second section why the idea won't work. Then the third person looks at the idea and the critique, and writes down how to improve the idea based on the critique so it can work. In this exercise, the initial idea gets critiqued and improved upon, and ownership moves beyond the first person.

The Gift Making Exchange
Start off a creative session by building
something small & momentous

9. The Gift Making Exchange

 The Use Case

When you need to get people in a creative, building mood, like at the start of a workshop.

 Team Ritual

This team ritual can be set to organizations as well.

 Props

+ Paper
+ Scissors
+ Tape

ı Any other prototyping material

 Difficulty Level

This is a low cost and low-planning ritual—you need basic materials ready for people to use.

What is the ritual?

Begin a creative session with a Gift Making Exchange to get the teammates into a generous, prototyping spirit. The ritual is simple to set up and launch. Have basic materials set up around the room: tape, paper, scissors, foil, clips, and anything else you have on hand.

Arrange people into small teams. Announce that each team will have 5 minutes to make a gift for the team on their right. They can use any material they have on them, or around the room. Encourage them to do something surprising or interactive. After 5 minutes, have a gift exchange, one team at a time. Everyone watches the gift exchange. Each team presents their gift, and the other team thanks them.

The ritual should help people warm up to one another—with small, meaningful gifts that show appreciation. It also sets an example of using basic materials to create something special. It should lower the barrier for further creative work during your time together.

The SKILL SHARE Fest

Everyone can share their secret MAKER SKILLS

10. The Skill-Share Fest

 The Use Case

When you need to bring out people's creative leadership.

 Org Ritual

This org ritual can be set to teams or divisions.

 Props

+ Schedule
+ Materials for activities
+ Appreciation or recognition
  props for the instructors

 Difficulty Level

This is a high-planning, medium cost event. You need to create time and resources for a day event, along with recognition materials.

What Is the Ritual?

The Skill-Share Fest is a day off from the normal work routine, where team members share their maker skills with one another in a festive environment. Everyone can teach the rest of their team how to cook a certain dish, build something, perform a dance, make a craft, or some other skill that they've developed. It's structured like an "unconference" where individuals can set the agenda by proposing sessions they'd like to offer, or those they'd like to attend.

The company Pinterest developed this ritual, around one of their core values of "knitting." They run a Knit Con that lets all of the employees share projects and skills they've developed, so people can learn from one another and create new things. It's a way to encourage employees to bring their "whole self" to work, and find hidden connections among team members—appreciating the talents they don't usually get to share at work.[28]

How It Works

Pinterest's design team created Knit Con with inspiration from other skill-sharing unconference events, where developers, designers, teachers, and journalists share their knowledge and strategies with each other in decentralized events. They created a basic infrastructure for the event, and then had the employees become the teachers to drive the schedule and content.

- Announce the SkillShare Fest, and invite all employees to be a "teacher" to share their secret skill with others.

- Create an online grid of times for the event day, with windows of 20 or 30 minutes. Share it with all the "teachers," for them to sign up for a window

- At the start of the day, do a warm-up—like a tournament of rock-scissors-paper—to help everyone mix together and build energy for the rest of the day.

- The backdrop in the central area should have the names of all the teachers listed on it—to show appreciation and focus on them as the 'heroes' of the event. All attendees also get a tote bag with the names of the teachers on it as well. And all teachers get an appreciation gift for leading a session.

- Mix the day's teaching events with social mixers, and food.

- Brand the day with visuals, and small experiential moments so employees feel the uniqueness of the day.

- Allow other pop-up events (like a board game tournament) to emerge—the employees should set the direction.

Some example skill shares might be how to make Boba tea, how to perform ballet moves, watercolor 101, making salsa, doing hula dancing, or pickling vegetables. The event should let employees' passions and talents shine—especially helping introverts to take the lead in setting the agenda.

How to Adapt

At Pinterest, Knit Con has happened for several years—growing each time to include thousands of employees. It was an unusual type of event to run, because the organizers had to give up control to the employees. But with a basic, "quiet" structure at the backbone of the event, they were able to recruit and support teachers to lead the sessions.

Participants ended up bonding with one another in magical ways—and also discovering hidden talents that didn't usually emerge in their usual work culture (which is not arrogant, and not bragging). It turned out that fellow employees were former ballerinas and athletes, skilled outdoorsmen and-women, and great cooks and artists.

Participants rated the event with highly positive reactions—never going below 95% approval. Especially as the company itself grew, the event helped to keep the culture strong and scale up the central ethos of the company. For many people, it was like "Pinterest in real life," with people sharing their hobbies, trying new ideas, and appreciating one anothers' skills.

Other companies might adapt the day-long Skill Share Festival to a smaller workshop, where people go around and quickly share a talent and teach it to the other attendees.

A key point for adaptation is to make the people sharing their skills into the "heroes"—spotlighting them, their contributions, and showing appreciation to them.

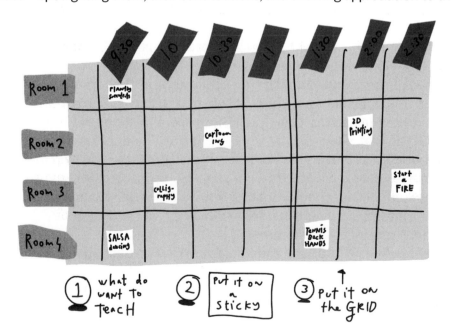

Laura Miner

Brand Designer
Founder BuddyBuddy Studio

Work on Rituals

Laura is a brand designer with a passion for people dynamics. She focuses on telling stories and making objects that support rituals.

Many of her rituals cross over into community building and advocacy. She designed and widely disseminated "Love Will Win" posters in early 2017 that made thousands of people march-ready for almost any protest.

For her kid's underrated elementary school, she wanted to change ingrained underdog behaviors in the up-and-coming school community. To do that, she created special sweatshirts and buttons for the school, so people could wear their "fandom" of the school. For an electric bike festival, she created the festival logo and identity and threw in some "car-free kid" buttons and stickers to encourage new transportation rituals among families.

Laura has found much of ritual creation to be in the framing. She discovered that design is really helpful when encouraging new behavior.

Learnings and Impact

Environments where the work is fast-paced and the change is constant create friction: reorgs, misunderstandings, frustrations. It's extremely important to counteract this friction with positive associations among team members. Quarterly offsites, team lunches and dinners, happy hours, and the like may seem frivolous but they are the opposite. She thinks of them like an oil change for the car. Skip them and your performance will decline and you will run the risk of more major repair down the line.

Backstory on Skill-Share Fest

About a decade ago Laura heard about an event called Foo Camp and her life and work was forever changed. Foo Camp is for technologists and other creative people to come together at an "unconference," where attendees set the schedule and lead events, with lots of spontaneity and flexibility built in. It was started in 2003 by Sara Winge and Tim O'Reilly at O'Reilly Publishing. What began as impromptu camping and conferencing for Friends of O'Reilly in their corporate offices spun into a much respected event for the best and brightest in tech to brain swap.

It also inspired countless other events, such as "Bar Camp," an open-to-the-public version of Foo Camp (named because of the programming slang term "foobar"). And it inspired many of Laura's own events.

When she fell in love with the concept of the Foo Camp and un-conferences, she didn't understand the nitty gritty of why attendee-led or skill-share events were so special. And maybe they didn't either. Maybe they just stumbled upon a formula that makes people feel seen, creates an alternative world where anyone can have a great idea, and relights a fire of passion within people.

It ended up being a particularly good fit for Pinterest, where Laura found the employees to be extremely high achieving. They have more passions than time and the culture is very non-assuming (read: bragging is poorly tolerated).

Knit Con (see the previous ritual description, for Skill Share Fest) allowed for the employees teaching classes to bring their whole selves to the office for the first time, and for all employees to experiment with new hobbies in an "offline Pinterest" kind of way.

Would she recommend an event like this to another organization or company? Absolutely. In her role running an event design studio, she frequently encourages solutions that help people feel heard, connect them to one another, help them take off their masks, and democratize knowledge. The details differ but the values don't.

Excitement for the Future of Work
During the first Knit Con they had an amazing speaker named Adam Steltzner from NASA. He was sort of a rockabilly scientist with a ton of wisdom to share, but the thing that stuck with her the most was his advice to imagine the best possible future and work towards it every day. Personally, she hopes to see fewer cars, more bikes, and more forests circling our cities—and she's really excited to live and work in that world.

4

Performance and Flow Rituals

Performance and flow rituals help people to deal with high-stakes work situations, cope with anxiety, and focus on getting to their goals. They can bring a sense of control in times of uncertainty—like during a big meeting, in the middle of a pitch or a trial, or when over-whelmed with too many deadlines.

Rituals' use of repetition and physical action help develop a sense of flow and confidence. Past research (see Chapter 1) shows that per-forming rituals helps people to regulate their emotions, decrease anxiety, and get into a flow state. Following the pattern of a ritual can also help people to block distractions, and set rules for themselves about how to work better.

When Would You Use a Performance Ritual?

Individual
+ Make you more focused
+ Eliminate distractions for deep work
+ Manage your emotions in a high stakes situation
+ Create a sense of control and boost confidence

Team
+ Rescue the team from distractions
+ Encourage forward motion with your projects
+ Recognize the team's purpose before a big event

Organization
+ Remove the distractions from the team calendar
+ Keep and maintain meaning purpose in your professional life
+ Pair buddies for increasing performance

10 Performance and Flow Rituals

11 The Focus Rock
Making Your Focus Tangible

12 Amp Up Rituals
Regulate Your Emotions Before a High-stake Situation

13 The Moment of Reverence
Acknowledge Your Purpose Before Starting a Big Task

14 Blind Writing
Eliminate Distractions for Creative Work

15 Touch Here for Special Powers
A Placebo to Charge People Up

16 The Airplane Mode Afternoon
Create a distraction-free zone for focus work

17 Six Daily Questions
A Regular Reminder of Your Focus

18 The To-Do Compost
Appreciate How Much You Accomplish

19 Silent Disco Thursdays
Nurturing a Culture of Flow & Deep Work

20 Partner Bonds
Pairs of Team Members Build Stronger Relationships

The FOCUS ROCK
MAKING YOUR FOCUS TANGIBLE

11. The Focus Rock

 The Use Case

When you need to focus on deep work, especially when you have too much flexibility and need to get difficult creative work done.

 Individual Ritual

Individual ritual—teams could do the same ritual in a designated time.

 Props

+ Focus rock (or similar object)
+ Headphones

 Difficulty Level

This is a low cost, low planning ritual.

What Is the Ritual?

The Focus Rock ritual is about using a prop—like a rock, or any other small item of your choice—to symbolize a dedication to being focused in your work.

It's an extraordinary simple ritual: put the rock on your work space, say your intention of what you want to accomplish, and then start your work. You can set a timer. The rule is that when the rock is there, you must stay focused. When the time or task is up, you thank the rock for helping you, and you put it away.

The rock should be a symbol of a special power. When it's on the table near you, it gives you energy to go into "deep flow" and forget about the rest of the world around you. You should use it selectively, so that it does not lose its power to keep you focused.

How It Works

The Focus Rock ritual brings a layer of intentionality and mind-setting to work that requires a great deal of focus—like writing, designing, and other creative work. It should help you make a special designated time for the tasks that often get put off in favor of shorter, less-deep tasks. The prop and intention of the ritual can especially help people who set their own time—like a student writing a PhD thesis—by creating rules they have to follow.

You can replace the rock with another prop—perhaps one that has a stronger symbolic meaning for you. You can also use a cube timer instead—that has a countdown included, so that you are physically setting a time for yourself to remain focused. The Rock as a key prop was the design of one of the students in our d.school ritual class—he chose it as something simple to have.

In addition, you might wear a special, bright pair of headphones while you are doing the Focus Rock ritual, to signal to others around you in a co-working or office space that you are doing deep work and should not be interrupted.

AMP UP RITUALS
Regulate your EMOTIONS Before a HIGH-STAKE situation

12. Amp-Up Rituals

 The Use Case

Before you are set to perform or present, in a high-stress or high-stakes situation.

 Individual & Team Ritual

This is an individual ritual, and can be done by teams as well.

 Props

+ It can be a word, mantra, or lyrics, or a physical object

 Difficulty Level

This is a low cost, low planning ritual.

What Is the Ritual?

Amp-Up rituals are small physical actions to take right before you are about to enter a high-stakes situation. They draw on athletes' practices before starting a match or a race. They are usually a small sequence of actions, sometimes combined with special words to repeat—all with the purpose of getting you in the right mindspace to be focused and successful when you enter into a space where you need to perform at a high level. This could be before a sales pitch, a negotiation, an executive meeting, or a presentation to a large group of people.

Research shows that amp-up rituals regulate your emotions and give you a sense of control.[29] When you state your intention at the start, you can increase your motivation and confidence.

How It Works

There are many amp-up rituals, from athlete's pre-match practices to actors' backstage warm-ups.[30]

One famous example is the Haka ritual practiced by New Zealand's rugby team. In the Haka ritual, the team comes onto the field, and the lead player begins shouting, "Prepare yourself.. This is the hairy man.. I die, I die, I live, I live." Other players repeat after him, while also moving in sync. The goal is to fire up the players, boost the team confidence, and intimidate the opponent. The ritual is rooted in a symbolic war dance of the Maori Aborigines. In Haka, the acts and sayings draw on emotions of anger, and joy.

Another example of an Amp Up ritual is ball-tossing among a team that is getting ready to make a presentation. The ball gets passed from person to person based on random prompts.

+ One person picks a category—like "name a food that is blue."
+ One person takes the ball and shouts an example that fits the category—like, "Blueberry."
+ Then they toss the ball to someone across the circle, and that person has to give another example, like, "Blue Raspberry Lollipops."
+ Continue the game until the category is exhausted, or until 2 minutes pass.
+ The goal of the ritual is to loosen up, feel connected, and help the team focus before the performance.

Ayse Birsel

Designer, Artist, Author
Birsel+Seck Studio

Work on Rituals

Ayse's work is all about utilizing her creative process of deconstruction and reconstruction, to help people enter their creative space quickly and easily. The rigor of her process structures people's creativity. It gets them over the anxiety and pressure about coming up with the best ideas from the get go. Instead, her work allows people to build towards great ideas step by step.

Rituals are key for this creative process. Ayse uses rituals to help people get into the right mental space, and she uses them in her own creative practice. Her daily drawing ritual is about getting over the fear of the blank, white page, with a quick, 2-3 minute drawing. (See more in Chapter 3.)

She also uses rituals to help bring out creative work from her clients. She has borrowed from Surrealist parlor games, like Exquisite Corpse, to do drawing games with client groups. The drawings grow into often surprising creations, while the ritual breaks the ice and gets people laughing together.

Another ritual strategy Ayse uses at the beginning of meetings is to have people introduce themselves and name their emotions. They're allowed to talk about whatever they are feeling at that moment, the good and the bad. People can share how they feel stressed about being stuck in traffic and arriving late for the meeting, or how excited they are or that they're feeling ambivalent about what they're going to do next. All emotions are welcome and the goal is to give people room to express themselves—release the emotion and move beyond it for a better meeting.

Lessons from Rituals at Work

Ayse has learned that rituals at work can help you get over your fears. Almost everything we do involves some fear, no matter of how experienced we are. Rituals gets you into the moment before you can overthink and worry about whatever it is you're doing. Rituals help you show up.

She says, "I learned a ritual from Marshall Goldsmith, my mentor, who is one of the world's top leadership coaches. He taught me to sing 'There's No Business Like Show Business,' at the start of every presentation, especially before going in front of an audience. Now it's become our ritual. I have my team huddle together—like a soccer or rugby team—and sing this song before we start any presentation. It pumps us up, reminds us to be present in the moment and sets the stage for us as performance of business. Having rituals makes you a little more fearless."

Excitement for Future of Work

With every technology, Ayse finds that we invent new rituals. Before there was recorded music, you couldn't listen to music and work at the same time. She remembers when her parents bought her a little portable TV for her room when she was growing up. She started doing her homework while she watched TV, which apparently is a terrible way to study.

Her design rituals used to be sketching in her Moleskine notebook with a black Pilot Bravo pen. Now it is sketching on her iPad with a stylus and a little black half-glove designed for drawing tablets. Next she might turn holograms of sketches into 3D space, with them hovering over a tablet—kind of like in a superhero movie.

The MOMENT of REVERENCE

Acknowledge your purpose before starting a big task

13. The Moment of Reverence

 The Use Case

Before you or your team is about to start an important procedure or talk.

 Team Ritual

This is a team ritual that can be set to individuals as well.

 Props

+ A word, or mantra

 Difficulty Level

This is a low-cost, low-planning ritual.

What Is the Ritual?

The Moment of Reverence is a short ritual that occurs right before an important event, meeting, or talk. It is taken from a hospital team practice at the Beth Israel Deaconess Medical Center.[31] Right before a surgery begins, the whole team of doctors, nurses, and others stop what they are doing. They take a short moment to remember the person on whom they are going to conduct the surgery.

The goal is to ensure that everyone remembers the humanity of the situation. It's about breaking the routine procedures, pausing to recognize the importance of what's happening, and appreciating the people involved. The moment can also reinforce the mindfulness that everyone should be proceeding with—to encourage care, precision, and empathy.

How It Works

In the case of a hospital procedure, the Moment of Reverence is carried out by a team during the run-up to the surgery at the Beth Israel Deaconess Medical Center.

- Before operating on a patient, the team pauses right after completing the pre-surgery checklist for a moment of reverence.

- The circulating nurse reminds everyone who the patient is, if they are someone's mother, father, sister, or brother, and to be considerate with the patient's needs.

- Everyone is silent during the moment.

- Once the set time is over, the team continues on with the medical work.

How to Adapt

The Moment of Reverence can also be an individual ritual. For example, author Clay Shirky takes intentional pauses while walking from his desk to a meeting. He takes a few meditative seconds to reflect on crossing over from one environment to the next.[32]

Taking a moment can help a person be conscious of the others around them, and the higher purpose of their work. It can also be a means to transition from one role to another. The ritual can help you to get into the headspace to perform tasks with more attention, empathy, and teamwork.

BLIND WRITING
Eliminate distractions for creative work

14. Blind Writing

 The Use Case

For writing projects that needs focus and self-awareness.

 Individual Ritual

This is an individual ritual, but it can be set to teams as well.

 Props

+ Computer
+ Word Processor
+ Music Playlist
+ Timer

 Difficulty Level

This is a low-cost, low-planning ritual.

What Is the Ritual?

Blind Writing is a ritual for when it feels impossible to tackle a big writing project that requires focus, detail, and creativity. Blind Writing removes one of the main barriers, the self-consciousness of what the words look like on the page.

Blind Writing is borrowed from art class warm-ups—when you do a contour-line sketch where you draw something in the room without looking down at your paper and without taking your pen off the surface.
Here, the ritual adapts the contour line drawing to writing. It's all about keeping your words moving and not looking down at what you're doing.

How It Works

The ritual is very simple—all you need is a computer, something to be writing, and the ability to turn your screen off while your computer is still on.

- Set a timer for 15 minutes, bring up your word processor, and queue up a music playlist that is around five songs long.

- Make sure your cursor is on the word processor application—so that if you start typing, words will be typed into it.

- Then turn the screen totally off while keeping your machine on. You should not be able to see anything on your screen.

- The challenge is, once you hit play on the music and the timer, you must keep writing for that 15 minutes.

- While the timer is going, you must keep typing throughout the songs. Try not think too much about what you're writing as long as you are moving your fingers. It's not about quality, just quantity!

- Once your time is over, you can turn the screen brightness back up, and see what you can use from the past 15 minutes worth of words. Cut, paste, salvage—and try to keep the state of flow going by continuing your work on the writing project.

The driving principle is that just doing something will loosen up your ability to get into creative flow. Turn off the pressure to be perfect while creating—and instead, just create, see what comes of it, and make use of what you can.

TOUCH HERE
A PLACEBO to CHARGE PEOPLE

15. Touch Here for Special Powers

 The Use Case

To create a touchstone in your workspace, for people to charge up their energy and confidence.

 Individual Ritual

This is an organizational ritual, can be set for individuals and teams.

 Props

+ Touch button
+ Canvas with a touch button image or drawing

 Difficulty Level

This is a low cost, low planning ritual.

What Is the Ritual?

Touch for Special Powers is a simple ritual to create an organization-wide symbolic action that inspires people to do great, quality work.

It takes its inspiration from the "Play Like a Champion" sign inside the University of Notre Dame football team's locker room. Each player touches the sign as they leave the locker room and go onto the field. It's a small ritual to charge people up.

The ritual prop—either with a similar sign, or with a button—doesn't pretend to actually imbue someone with a special power. It is all about the placebo effect, of giving people a sense of control, combined with a hint of magic.

How It Works

● Craft the message of your special power button or sign. You can put a phrase around it—taking inspiration from others like "Touch Here for Special Powers" or "Play Like a Champion Today."

● Make the thing. You could draw or print it, frame it, and hang it on the wall. Or you could make it more tactile, like a button or a special prop that you can put on the wall or a special place.

● Choose a space to put it where organization members pass by daily, so that it becomes part of the routine flow. It could be by the coffee machine, the elevators, or the water fountain. The goal is that a wide selection of people get used to it as a touchstone, and it becomes part of an everyday habit to get inspired and empowered.

● For a team, you can integrate the Special Powers button in both ordinary situations like a stand-up meeting, or for bigger events like kicking off a new project.

The Airplane Mode Afternoon
Create a distraction-free zone for focused work

16. The Airplane Mode Afternoon

 The Use Case

When deep work needs to be done by a team, to make progress on hard tasks.

 Team Ritual

This is a team ritual that individuals can use.

 Props

+ Focus Cards
+ Computers

 Difficulty Level

This is a low-cost, low-planning ritual.

What Is the Ritual?
Airplane Mode Afternoon is a simple flow ritual for people to create a distraction-free zone for work.

This ritual is meant to capture the special environment of an airplane, where many of the typical external distractions are blocked by the lack of Internet connection. The ritual is about recreating a version of this, with a temporary block on web browsing, notifications, and social media.

While clearing out Internet distractions, this ritual aims to get a person or a team to a deeper level of focus. It's about making an environment of a "captive audience" for a limited time period, to have everyone collectively agree to eliminate distractions and force themselves to make progress on especially hard tasks.

How It Works

- Everyone should be gathered together for the afternoon, ready with a "Focus Task" to work on by themselves. You can have each person write down this task on a special piece of paper.

- The story is that everyone is a passenger on a fictional plane ride together.

- One person is the afternoon's host. This person is responsible for asking everyone to turn off the Wifi on their devices, and making a walk-around, just like a on a plane. They can also pick the destination for the day.

- At the host's announcement, everyone initiates the airplane mode by disconnecting from their Wifi.

- If the host likes, they can add white noise to mimic the airplane feel.

- Set the "flight time"—minimum of 45 minutes.

- Once the time is up, the host announces arrival, and that Wifi can be turned back on. Just like when some planes land, there can be clapping for a safe arrival.

SiX DAiLY QuestioNs
A regulaR ReMiNDer of YouR FoCuS

17. Six Daily Questions

 The Use Case

When you want to create awareness, a sense of control, and focus
for personal and professional
goals.

 Individual Ritual

This is an individual ritual.

 Props

+ Reminders—physical, digital,
  interpersonal

 Difficulty Level

This is a low-cost, low-planning
ritual.

What Is the Ritual?
Six Daily Questions is an individual ritual to remind yourself of your goals
and life priorities on a daily basis.

Marshall Goldsmith designed this ritual to keep himself focused on his
primary goals.[33] Everyday, at the same time, he arranges for someone to call
him. They ask him the same six questions every day (that he wrote himself,
for himself):

+ Did you do your best to set clear goals?
+ To make progress on those goals?
+ To find meaning?

+ To be engaged?
+ To be happy?
+ To build good relationships?

The person on the other side just listens without judgment, and says encouragement words before hanging up.

How it works
Behavior change is hard. It needs goal-setting, awareness, and a persistent attitude. Six Daily Questions is a daily reminder ritual to help individuals get there.

● Come up with six questions that you would like to answer on a daily basis. If you are not sure where to start, begin with Marshall's themes: setting goals, being happy, building strong relationships, and being engaged.

● Ask a person to ask you these questions every day—or set a daily reminder for yourself.

● If you have another person to ask you the questions, answer the questions at the same time everyday. If you are answering solo, write them down. Be sure to hold yourself accountable.

● After some time, have a checkpoint to see where you are. Have you kept up with asking/answering the questions? Do you see any progress in your responses?

● If you have made progress, give yourself a small gift—a nice lunch, a break from work, or a new book. Celebrate by giving yourself small experiential gifts when you have made progress.

Marshall Goldsmith evolved the daily questions over time. He tweaked the questions from regular questions to active questions. For example, he went from "Did I set clear goals?" to "Did I do my best to set clear goals?" This small tweak increases the ownership and engagement for the person who is answering the questions.

Based on approximately five thousand surveys, Marshall discovered some insights on the effectiveness of six daily questions. By active self-questioning, people become more aware of where they are in their endeavor. This awareness increases their sense of control and responsibility. Awareness has the potential to spark change and persistence in making the change.

Dr. Marshall Goldsmith

Business Educator and Coach

Work on rituals

Marshall's work in coaching people in their work has led him to conclude that people need very clear and structured rituals to get much of anything done.

This applies to all areas of people's life: from leadership, to health care, to family relationships.

Marshall developed the practice of Six Daily Questions (see the previous ritual) with his daughter, Dr. Kelly Goldsmith who is a Professor at Vanderbilt. In her research in marketing and organizations, she identified that almost all research on employee engagement revolved around "passive questions"—such as "Do you have meaningful work?" When people are asked passive questions, they invariably blame their problems on the environment.

From this insight came the idea of bringing active questions into work life. They crafted the Daily Question ritual with active questions that begin with "Did I do my best to..." These questions aim to get people to take responsibility, and to do it as a daily, iterative practice. They've found the ritual to have amazing results.

Suggestions to others to create better communities and culture

Marshall draws on insights about organizations from Peter Drucker: that in order to maximize your impact in an organization, including its culture, you need to win over the key decision makers. That means accepting and making peace with the fact that key decisions are made by people who hold the power. If an employee wants to change how an organization, it's crucial to present ideas well, and to focus on the future.

Excitement for the Future of work

Marshall has a new project about work and retirement. It's called "100

Coaches." It's a way to go beyond work and retirement—and build a lasting legacy for the future.

A couple of years ago, he attended a program led by designer Ayse Birsel (also profiled in this book in Chapter 4), called Design the Life You Love. At the program, Ayse asked everyone to write down the names of people's heroes.

Marshall wrote down Frances Hesselbein (former CEO of the Girl Scouts and recipient of the Presidential Medal of Freedom), Alan Mulally (former CEO of Ford and CEO of the year in the United States), Dr. Jim Kim (President of the World Bank), Peter Drucker (founder of modern management), Paul Hersey (noted author, teacher, and personal mentor of mine), and Warren Bennis

(one of the world's greatest leadership thinkers of his time). Then Ayse asked them to describe what made them think of them as heroes. Marshall wrote that they were all "great teachers" and "very generous." She then challenged the participants to "be more like them" in designing the lives we love.

It was from this program that Marshall came up with the idea to teach 15 people everything he knows at no charge. In return, these 15 would 'pay if forward' by doing the same thing for 15 others, for free. He was inspired to do this by the many great teachers and leaders who have so generously helped him—without ever asking for anything in return. It is his way of recognizing the amazing contributions they have made in his life.

The TO-DO COMPOST
Appreciate how much you accomplish

18. The To-Do Compost

The Use Case

When you need to get through many tasks to relieve the stress of a long to-do list, and establish a sense of a progress.

Individual Ritual

This is an individual ritual, but it can be set to teams as well.

Props

+ Stickies to write your to-dos
+ Transparent container for your compost

Difficulty Level

This is a low-cost, low-planning ritual.

What Is the Ritual?

The To-Do Compost is a ritual to visualize your progress on your to-do list in a more tangible rewarding way. You write down your to-dos on sticky notes—one per note. Then when you complete a task, you physically tear it up and add it to your compost jar.

As your to-dos get composted, you will see their shreds rise. It's a physical measure of getting work done. By feeding your compost with completed tasks and visually seeing your progress, you can decrease the anxiety and stress that comes with completing them. This is a playful way of crossing off a long, scary list.

How It Works

- During one of your stressed-out working sessions, lay out all the tasks that are stressing you out, including big and small things.

- Set a measuring cup or other transparent container. Set it next to your workspace.

- List out all your to-dos, usually six to ten, on stickies on your desk.

- Get to work—taking one sticky at a time, and putting it as your central focus.

- Once you get through that sticky task, you, tear it up into tiny little bits and put it in your cup.

- Have the cup up on your workspace all the time. You can see the amount of stuff that you have done, physically measuring more.

- Once you reach the top, burn the completed to-dos or send them to the recycling bin.

- Celebrate it with a giant stress smoothie or a dessert of your choice.

You can create a team version of this ritual by adding several steps. First co-write all the to-dos of the week on Monday morning or whatever your team cycle suggests. Pick a common area for the To-Do Compost.

Alternatively, team members can take the to-dos that they are supposed to work on. Whenever someone finishes the task, that person goes to the To-Do Compost Wall and tears it up on the spot. If someone is around and sees the tearing up, they can congratulate you: "One less to go!" When it comes to the last to-do and it's ready to tear up, a team member calls for the to-do completion ceremony. The team tears up the last one together, and takes the to-do compost to the recycling bin. They celebrate with coffee or drinks.

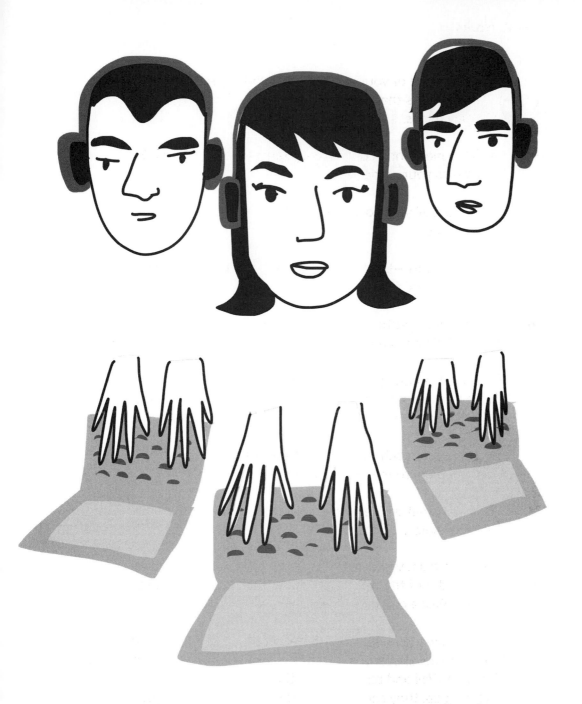

SILENT DISCO THURSDAYs
Nurturing a culture of FLOW + DEEP WORK

19. Silent Disco Thursdays

 The Use Case

When you want to nurture a culture of flow, and get team members to do deep, heads-down work.

 Team Ritual

This is a team ritual, can be set to departments and orgs as well.

 Props

+ Music, Earphones
+ Physical/Digital Reminders
+ Initiation and Ending props

 Difficulty Level

This is a low cost, low planning ritual.

What Is the Ritual?

Silent Disco Thursdays is a group ritual for employees who want to do heads-down work without meetings and distractions. During a set time, everyone is silent and listening to their favorite music.

The ritual is meant to rescue teams from meetings and the fatigue that comes with interruptions, distractions, and small interactions.

How it Works

Every Thursday, employees who want to join can come to the silent disco area, grab their headphones, and do their work as if they are at a party. Just like at Silent Discos in other contexts, the central organizers can broadcast a few channels of music, and everyone can choose on their headphones which channel to listen to.

They can switch music channels during the work party, or they can choose their own music stream. The shared music is one of the ritual elements, to sync people up in their individual focus, side by side.

How to Adapt
You can make other variations of the Silent Disco, that don't involve music but that have some other kind of strict rule to increase performance. The basic formula is to choose a restriction and a limited time, to make a ritual that will disrupt the default of too many meetings and distractions.

For example, the software company Asana has No Meeting Wednesdays to increase productivity and make employees happier.[34] No one is allowed to schedule a meeting on the given day of the week. This means that at least one day of the week should be uninterrupted, flow-friendly work for everyone in the office.

No Talk Days are another version. There's no disco music, instead just a rule that no one can talk in the office during the day. Jason Fried, the co-founder of the software company 37signals (that makes Basecamp) proposed a No Talk day every week to encourage more focused accomplishments.[35]

20. The Partner Bonds

 The Use Case

When you want to build better partnerships between individuals who have been paired together on a project.

 Team Ritual

This is a team ritual, to be co-created by pairs together.

 Props

+ Mantra
+ Secret handshakes
+ Small gifts to give

 Difficulty Level

This is a low-cost, low-planning ritual.

What is the ritual?

Partner Bonds are rituals that you can encourage pairs in your teams to build together. They are one-to-one, usually secret actions that team partners can develop together.

Strong partnerships at work can help unite people with different skill sets and seniority levels. Some companies, like Pinterest and SYPartners, deliberately pair up individuals, for a few weeks at a time. The pairs can work near each other, support each other in their projects, and hold each other accountable.

Rituals like secret handshakes, mantras, and small gift-giving can bring people together more quickly. The bonding will help them to build a relationship in which they trust each other and feel safe to be honest, critical, and creative together.

How It Works
Even if people are on the same team, this ritual gives them the chance to get to know each other better, and to find untapped connections and aspirations.

Setting up this ritual is useful when you have a team that you want to perform better. It can be especially useful when you have tasks that require multiple skill sets. Or when you have a mix of junior and senior team members who can learn from each other. It can also lead to creativity when you are exploring new horizons for your team and need orthogonal ideas.

Pairing team members is proven to be an effective way to increase team performance and output.[36] In our research, we also discovered that consultancies like SYPartners,[37] and tech companies like Pinterest are actively using pairing employees in their team life.[38]

5

Conflict and Resilience Rituals

Conflicts are an inevitable part of work life—as are failures. Both can bring intense emotions and possibly destroy relationships.

Rituals can be strategies to navigate conflicts, to manage anger and frustration, and to move towards a more constructive relationship.

Ideally, they can structure spaces for more candid, transparent communication—as well as personal resilience to deal with mistakes. They bring awareness, reflection, and mindfulness to increase people's ability to manage negative things at work.

When Would You Use a Conflict & Resilience Ritual?

Individual
+ Help team members to avoid clashes
+ Decrease anxiety before high-stake feedback sessions
+ Proactively prevent burnout

Team
+ Nurture radical transparency to avoid clashes
+ Take an intentional pause from a heated discussion
+ Resolve a conflict by letting emotions free
+ Prevent conflicts related to project priorities

Organization
+ Nurture a culture of candor
+ Build psychological safety with team members
+ Address team health issues with a neutral party

10 Conflict and Resilience Rituals

21 The Doctor Is In
When You Need to Address Unstated Problems

22 The Community Conversations
Nurture Candor for Healthy Relationships

23 Robot Walkout
Take a Pause from a Heated Discussion

24 The Anxiety Wall
Lower Stress before a Performance Review

25 Burn the Argument
Resolve a Conflict by Letting Emotions Free

26 Elephant, Dead Fish, Vomit
Bring Out People's Candor and Resilience

27 My First Failure Book
Embrace Vulnerability with New Team Members

28 No Rehash Rule
Nudge Team Members to Move On

29 Trade-off Sliders
Prevent Conflicts Around Priorities and Resources

30 The Small Moments Jar
Repair Relationships with Small Appreciations

The DOCTOR Is IN
WHEN you NEED to ADDRESS UNStated
                              PROBLEMS

21. The Doctor is In

 The Use Case

When teams have been working together for a while, and problematic dynamics emerge, this ritual can help find and address them.

 Team Ritual

This is a team ritual.

 Props

+ Room for the event
+ Props for doctor role
+ Coffee and snacks

 Difficulty Level

This calls for a charismatic instigator, with very strong facilitation skills and the seniority and credibility to get teams to accept the invitation. This also needs a culture open to trying new things.

What Is the Ritual?

The Doctor Is In is a ritual for reflecting on team dynamics and making a space for new practices.[39] It's a pop-up space, in which one person in your organization plays a doctor for other teams.

Any team that needs to address a recurring or one-off issue, can get a one-hour consultation from this doctor. The doctor will be a neutral internal facilitator who helps the team by facilitating a conversation around the issue. The doctor won't disclose the conversation to anyone outside the team. The meeting might entail the team mapping out and prioritizing the issue, building alignment between team members, and plans to establish stronger relationships.

How It Works

This ritual was developed at the software company Atlassian, by Dom Price. He started having one-hour coffee conversations with others' teams, in which he facilitated them talking about what was going wrong with the team and what needed to be addressed. Seeing how popular these sessions were, he then formalized it into a doctor's visit.

He got a doctor's outfit, put up posters around the office inviting teams to come for a visit, and blocked off a meeting room for a week. Anyone who wanted to bring a team could come to talk for one hour. There would be no discussion of Key Performance Indicators or performance reviews. The teams could also trust that there would be doctor's confidentiality—nothing would be sent up for management to hear.

The goal was to have a "Health Monitor" session, in which the doctor could help a team be more honest with one another, and also design their own solutions to the dysfunctions they saw. The doctor-facilitator uses whiteboards, stickies, and other visualizations to push forward the discussions. But the doctor is not going to "fix" the problems—that is up to the team itself. At Atlassian, during the Doctor Is In week, "Doctor Dom" conducted 42 sessions with teams. He learned that there were particular roles that a facilitator could play with teams. First, the doctor should balance out the "celebrity" status of the alphas or leaders in the team, to ensure they don't dominate the discussion. The doctor can also ensure introverts are included, by holding some silent reflection and rating activities at the beginning of the session. This ensures that all will participate, and no one will be over influenced by others, when voicing what their priorities are.

The ritual can be adapted, perhaps to be a quarterly event, in which teams reflect about whether they should be going for Team Health Check-in. It's not recommended to be a mandatory checkup, but rather that teams should opt in. The "doctor" doesn't have to fully dress up like a doctor if they don't want to, but they should be trained in group or design facilitation to ensure the environment is constructive, empathetic, and balanced.

Dom Price
Work Futurist at Atlassian

Work on Rituals

When hired at Atlassian, Dom was tasked with identifying what they did well as a company and how they could replicate that across teams. At that point, the design team was already creating a team playbook to guide team culture. Dom joined them, and worked with them to develop a health monitor for assessing teams' wellbeing. Based on the health monitor, they created the Doctor Is In ritual.

Dom set up the doctor's ritual as a way to roll out the health monitor, and to also learn what the burning issues for teams in his company were. As he learned from the Doctor Is In sessions, he took on a facilitator role. He helped teams move towards solutions, using the playbook that the team was developing. He closes the Doctor's meetings with a commitment— asking each team members what action items they'll work on and what they'll do before the next session.

Dom held 42 sessions of Doctor Is In within one week. After that success, he took it on the road and has run it with over 2000 teams inside the company and out.

Learnings from Rituals at Work

The Doctor Is In ritual has become a regular tool for teams, even without Dom as a facilitator. It became a muscle that the company could deploy across the organization—so that there was no dependency on a single key individual. This is a success: spreading people's ability to run it themselves, and adapt it to their own practices.

Dom also found the power in structuring team meetings—and difficult conversations that are around conflicts and problems—so that they become safe and empowering for teams.

Most of the issues that teams were struggling with were common sense, very fixable, and not that surprising. But it took a frank and ritualized meeting to get them spoken out loud. The ritual version of the difficult conversation helped teams to own their continual improvement.

Suggestion to others for better communities and culture

Dom recommends that other companies who want to create their own rituals should fall in love with the problem before jumping to a solution. It also might mean stopping other practices to make room for new ones. Often companies' buckets are already full, and so it's worth reflecting on what behaviors or events need to end for something new to begin.

Another insight Dom has is not to hunt down "best practice"—because it doesn't exist. Rather, use agile tools, like design thinking, a business model canvas, and other practices, to build new culture strategies.

There are no silver bullets. Companies need to invest in understanding their environment—including their culture, values, people, skills, personality types, products, locations, time zones, expertise, customers, pace of change, innovation etc. Make sure that what you try works for you.

A final message from Dom: don't try to spread culture (or rituals) through mandate. A plan that has an official rollout likely will not work well. Let people come, have them direct it, and have them adapt it to their own needs. Otherwise, you will just get compliance—and not a healthy team.

COMMUNITY CONVERSATIONS
NURTURE CANDOR for healthy RELATIONSHIPS

22. Community Conversations

 The Use Case

When there are rumblings, gossip, and back channel frustrations being expressed about a recent decision or event.

 Org Ritual

This is an organizational ritual, can be set to teams.

 Props

+ Circular room
+ Note taking

 Difficulty Level

Need for a charismatic instigator, and an open-culture for trying new things.

What Is the Ritual?

The Community Conversations is an as-needed ritual, that can be held where there are frustrations brewing in the organization. The Conversation is a special kind of meeting. There are ground rules: that people should speak with radical candor about what is going on; that gossip and emotional breakdowns should be called out directly; and that the ultimate goal is to reconstruct the organizations' social fabric. The design agency IDEO developed this ritual to hold difficult conversations.

This Conversation can be useful for when a long-time, much-loved team member has been let go, and now employees are speculating about what happened. Or it could when there is gossip about reorganizations or austerity plans. A leader can call the Conversation to address these issues, or others can call for one to get more honest, open information.

How It Works

To hold a Community Conversation, there should be a particular theme or event it is responding to. Once you hold one Conversation, and communicate the rules and culture that people should expect, then it will become a more established mode of dealing with problems rumbling in the organization.

The Conversation should also be optional. All who come should be there voluntarily—and they should all formally acknowledge and commit to the rules that govern it.

While it started as a way to address a conflict, Community Conversations serve other purposes. It creates a safe environment where people can talk about important matters such as inclusion, and diversity in a more open and authentic way.

- Identify the topic for the Conversation. Find a space that will be intimate. It should allow for circular seating. It shouldn't hold too many people. The space should be a little cramped, so that people are close to each other, and that not too many people can come.

- Issue an invitation, that welcomes anyone who would like to talk about and address the topic to attend.

- The Conversation is first-come, first-seated—there are no reserved seats, and once the capacity is reached, then no one else can join.

- A facilitator should set the ground rules, and everyone should acknowledge that they understand them and will abide by them. **Vegas Rule**: What happens in Vegas stays in Vegas. If you want to say something that you don't want repeated, say "Vegas Rule" along with your comment. **Artichoke Rule**: Once a point has been made, there is no need for it to be repeated (by the same person or another). If it's getting reraised, others can call it out—saying "Artichoke" to move on. **Radical Candor Rules**: Don't talk "around" an issue—get to the honest, crucial things. Be direct, though do not be cruel.

- The timer is set for 1 hour. The conversation must end then. The facilitator will take notes (not to be shared)—and document the outcomes and accountability items that emerge. The outcomes, and accountability list will be shared with the rest of the organization, to ensure the conversation moves solutions forward.

23. Robot Walkout

 The Use Case

When a meeting ends up going awry—a disagreement arises and doesn't get resolved.

 Team Ritual

This is a team ritual that can be set to pairs inside the team.

 Props

An exit signal that the team needs to set up

 Difficulty Level

This is a low planning, spontaneous ritual that still needs to be established in a team.

What Is the Ritual?

Robot Walkout is useful as an "exit strategy" for a conversation that has become unproductive. This ritual signals that the initiator has recognized the stalemate and commits to come back to find a resolution at a later time. This can be accomplished by walking stiffly backwards like a robot while beeping.

If not a fan of robots, a team can come up with their own unique "exit signal." The team agrees that if a meeting is not going well, tempers are hot, or the problem seems intractable and simply needs a rest, then anyone can use this motion to signal an end to the meeting.

How it works

The Walk Out Ritual is one that depends on pre-planning in your team.

What will you define to be your agreed-upon Exit Signal? Ideally, it should be a little unusual and humorous, so that it can lighten a heavy discussion.

Once you set the Exit Signal, then any team-member is allowed to invoke it and all others must follow. Then the ritual will proceed as follows, to pause the conversation and reset for later on.

- Once a meeting has clearly gone to a place that's not productive and on the verge of breaking down further—that's the trigger.

- One person can initiate the Walk Out by standing up and using the Exit Signal. For example, with the Robot Walkout, one person slowly walks backwards like a robot—stiff, beep, beep, beep.

- The other people must follow suit—the meeting is over, everyone stops talking. They can also do the signal too, to acknowledge that the meeting has broken down. They could also stand up and walk backwards like a robot.

- Once you're out of the meeting, you should go back to normal work—the meeting is done, and the problem is set aside for now.

- Once there's a cooling off period, the team can regroup and try again to resolve the problem that had derailed them.

This ritual came from Anima LaVoy, who uses it to break the tension and add some humor into tense discussions. The goal is to anticipate tensions will arise and to plan a constructive behavior to fall back on when that happens.

Anima LaVoy

Social Impact Experiences
Lead at Airbnb

Prior to her work at Airbnb, Anima was co-founder and Chief Product Officer of Connect, a tech platform that helps people manage their real-world social relationships. As part of her research, Anima collected hundreds of examples of the artful ways in which people build and nurture relationships in the workplace as well as in their families, friendships, and marriages. She sees the quality of our relationships as foundational to the quality of our lives, and believes "social health" should receive the same attention as physical health. Anima has been experimenting with relationship hacks and rituals such as job hats, gratitude jars, role maps, and robot walkouts.

It's about coming up with intentional and artistic hacks, practices, and rituals to live life better. This means for relationships from marriages and partnerships, to tech and design teams, to families and friends. All of

these feed into our "social health." Our interior lives are hard to talk about. We don't have a vocabulary to talk about it, and it's hard to quantify them. But they have a huge impact on our happiness and our longevity. Anima is focused on how we make real, quality social connections with people, with a focus not just on romantic relationships but all of the other relationships that contribute to our day-to-day lives.

For Anima, the focus is on interior potential. She has been working on how to bring more thoughtfulness, playfulness, and intentional strategies for her team's work lives. It's not about one single strategy to make relationships better. It's about an ecosystem of small behaviors that add up to meaning and connection. Anima connects relationship practices across the different circles in our lives—connecting work, to marriage, to family, to friends, and to neighbors, too.

The ANXIETy WALL
Lower stress Before a Performance review

24. The Anxiety Wall

 The Use Case

Before a performance review, when most team members feel anxious about what to expect.

 Team Ritual

This is a team ritual that can be set for orgs.

 Props

+ A canvas, tarpaulin, or other covering to protect the wall
+ Modeling clay or putty

 Difficulty Level

Low-planning ritual that requires one free wall.

What Is the Ritual?

The Anxiety Wall is a physical space for getting a team's collective anxieties out. It's meant for high-stress times, like around annual performance reviews, a reorganization, or a busy season.

A leader should find a wall that most people pass by, or that's directly close to "high-stress" places, like the meeting rooms where performance reviews will be held. The wall is a place where people can stick up little pieces of modeling clay to represent their nerves. They can play around with the dough while they are waiting to be called in, and then stick it up on the wall when it's their time.

It allows for nervous fiddling—giving a common action to perform to release worried energy. And it helps build a sense of shared emotions by showing that many others have similar feelings.

How It Works
An Anxiety Wall is a collective, simple ritual to deal with the stress that many are going through. One context can be annual performance reviews, where everyone in the organization will be receiving critiques. With that all of the possible critical feedback, people's nerves are on edge.

- Right near where the performance reviews will be happening—like outside the conference rooms that people will be meeting—find a space for the Wall to be set up. If you don't have a blank wall, you can set up a large whiteboard or another temporary wall covering there instead.

- Cover the wall in a durable surface, which people can stick things onto and write onto, without getting in trouble. It could be whiteboard paint, a large canvas, tarpaulin, or otherwise.

- Write "Anxiety Wall" on it, and leave simple instructions:
    Take some sticky stuff.
    Play while you wait. Roll it, smash it, twist it, whatever.
    When you're called in, stick it on the wall.
    Feel free to sign and write a message too.

- Set up a station with modeling clay or putty. Offer different colors for people to choose from.

- Watch the Wall grow. If you can keep it permanently, let it stay year to year, so that people can see it—and feel connected to all the people who came before them (and were also stressed out).

- If you have to take it down, make sure to take a photo of the Wall, and hang up the photo to keep the idea alive.

BURN the ARGUMENT
RESOLVE a CONFLICT by Letting the EMOTIONS FREE

25. Burn the Argument

 The Use Case

When a conflict arises, and team members feel burnt out from negativity.

 Team Ritual

This is a person-to-person ritual that can be also run with a team.

 Props

+ Heat-proof container
+ Stickies
+ Pen
+ Shredder
+ Matches

 Difficulty Level

This medium-planning ritual needs a neutral party to facilitate it, and it needs some props for the destruction.

What Is the Ritual?

Burn the Argument is a ritual to move people past a conflict that flared up. After a conflict has arisen among team members, have them release their emotional energy by symbolically burning their feelings.

Instead of hoping that the people will be able to move on after the argument, have them explicitly write down what they were arguing about, and what their feelings are. Make sure that they hear each other's point of view. Then have them put these written-down accounts and emotions into a shredder—or have them tear them up. They combine both of their scraps together, and burn them in a heatproof container.

The goal is to have the symbolic actions translate into real forgiveness, in which the people agree to move forward and to acknowledge each other's points of view.

How It Works

This ritual comes from the work of designer Lillian Tong (see her profile on the next page). She created it with the MakeShift co-working space to build forgiveness strategies into teams that worked there.[40]

Once an argument has happened, let the conflict cool down for a day or two. Ask the people who were arguing if they would be open to having a resolution meeting, to move past what happened. If they say yes, then organize the ritual.

- Invite anyone who was involved with the argument to come together. This could be just the people who were most involved, or it could also be other team members who were in the meeting where the argument happened.

- Everyone gets a stack of stickies and a marker. Ask them to write down what and how they are feeling, one thought per sticky. They should post them up on the wall or on the table, so that people can see them if they like.

- Once everyone is done, ask each person to silently reflect on how they might move past the argument. Give them one minute, and then ask them to let it go silently.

- Then ask them tear down the stickies, and either put them through a shredder or tear them up in pieces. Then everyone puts them into the box together.

- If your setup allows, take the box outside, to a barbecue or other safe place. Light it on fire, and watch it burn together. If you don't have a place to do this outside, place the paper scraps in a heatproof container in a safe place and burn them there.

- The ritual is over—and hopefully the argument is resolved and the team can move on.

Lillian Tong

Designer, Co-founder
Matter-Mind Studio

Work on Rituals

Lillian was doing her thesis project on emotions at work. She found that most people, when they work on this topic of emotions, direct their focus on "creating joy." This approach ends up creating things like Ping-Pong tables in a break room.

Instead, Lillian sees an opportunity to design around complex, negative emotions in the workplace. In her research, she found a trove of stories about how hard it is to express emotions at work. If you are getting emotional at work, you are seen as less professional. This leads to anxiety and conflict over how to mask these emotions, while still dealing with negative experiences that range from arguments with co-workers, to disappointing feedback, to overwheming demands, and to disrespectful treatment by superiors.

Lillian ran her thesis project as a "Ritual Design Consultancy" in which she worked with startups and co-working spaces to create rituals for them. She researched their values and cultures, and made "speculative" designs to stretch what might be possible in how they work in their teams. Some of those rituals ended up being installed for pilot runs, to test them out.

Learnings about Rituals at Work

Lillian has found ways through her design research to approach conflicts, stress, and other negative emotions at work. She uses these objects or activities to signal to people that it's okay to be emotional and still be professional. Rituals can be ways to acknowledge negative feelings about your own work, or with your co-workers, and to work through them.

In particular, she was looking at what emotions would cultivate creativity. Boredom is part of that, curiosity is part of that. So is feeling like you are an equal in a collaborative relationship, rather than in a hierarchy. Those are keys to making people feel confident.

During her Ritual Design Consultancy project, she was working with a startup as a client. She ran future workshops, to see what scenarios and emotions they would want to see in the future. She also researched what kind of learnings had been reviewed in the psychology studies about those emotions. When working on collaborative projects, people sitting at the same height are more likely to feel equal to each other. When they wear the same thing, it also helps. That inspired the "cocoon meeting" ritual design. In this, meetings happen on the ground, in a connected space. The goal is to help people get in sync.

Lillian found rituals to be one strong tool to design workplaces for people's emotional needs. Designers traditionally design physical or digital objects, or services. But rituals have a unique mindfulness, purpose, and intentionality built into them.

A workplace ritual has emotional components, that can be at different levels, for an inividual or a team.

Excitement for Future of Work
With more people working in the gig economy, and people working anywhere, this means that we need to figure out ways to bond people when they are remote. Lillian is considering this in her design work: when you are not in the same place as your co-workers, how do you build deeper connections? And when you are working by yourself, only communicating through screens, then people will also have more emotional needs—frustration, dislocation, miscommunication. We need new ways to build that sense of team—and to fight loneliness
.

This vision of future work also means that inside companies, there needs to be more people who are working on culture. These growing challenges need someone who is spending time to understand what is going on in the community, what values and dynamics are at work, and creating new rituals, events, and other strategies to build strong relationships.

ELEPHANT, DEAD FISH, VOMIT
Bring out PEOPLE's CANDOR & ReSILIENCE

26. Elephant, Dead Fish, Vomit

 The Use Case

When you want to nurture more honest dialogue among people about how the organization's work is going.

 Org Ritual

This is an org ritual that teams can use as well.

 Props

+ The select phrase for triggering the conversation

 Difficulty Level

Low-planning—it's setting up a conversation in a better way.

What Is the Ritual?

When you want to encourage reciprocal, honest conversations among team members across an organization, try the ritual Elephant, Dead Fish, Vomit. This is a way to interrupt a meeting that doesn't seem to be "honest" enough, and to structure a conversation to deal with issues that people cannot seem to get over, or that they're struggling to express to each other

Anyone can say the phrase "Elephant, dead fish, and vomit." Then everyone in the meeting gets permission to speak their mind in a safe environment, about big things in the room that are not being addressed (elephants); about things that are long past but still haunting the group (dead fish); and about things people just need to vent out without real goals (vomit).

How It Works

This ritual was developed at Airbnb, to try to build a more open and honest working culture.[41] One of the founders, Joe Gebbia, proposed this as a way to get from one-way organization-wide talks, to more two-way conversations. This honesty is part of the company's core values, and the ritual is one way to possibly make it real.

The idea for the ritual arose after the results of a company-wide survey showed that employees thought the company needed work on openness and honesty. The idea was to have an Elephant, Dead Fish, Vomit conversation at an all-hands meetings, to prompt better dialogue.

- At a team or organization meeting, introduce the triad: that anyone can say the phrase "Elephant, Dead Fish, Vomit"— or a single one of the words—to signal that it's time to have a more candid conversation.

- The term "Elephant" should call people out to talk about the big things that people are worried about, but they're not talking about. It could be an impending change, a big piece of bad news, or something embarrassing.

- "Dead Fish" should help people identify old issues that won't go away—and hopefully, by calling them out, explicitly task the group to move past them (or at least recognize that they keep calling back to things in the past).

- "Vomit" is a flag for anyone who just needs to vent about something that is a big deal for them, even if they don't know exactly what "it" is.

- When anyone invokes all three, then the whole team should share any of the points that need to be raised, to get to a more honest conversation.

- Or a person can raise a single, potentially uncomfortable point by phrasing it as an Elephant, a Dead Fish, or Vomit. The rest of the group should recognize the signal. They can think about what else they could add in that mode.

MY FIRST FAILURE BOOK

Embrace vulnerability with new team members

27. My First Failure Book

 The Use Case

When you want to instill a sense of safety among employees, especially junior ones.

 Team Ritual

This is a team ritual that can be made into an organization one.

 Props

+ A book that can grow, and be filled with examples and clippings, like a scrapbook

 Difficulty Level

The medium-planning ritual requires initial research and documentation of failures.

What Is the Ritual?

The First Failure Book aims to create more honesty and a sense of safety among team members. It's a growing collection of stories from employees about how they have failed while at this job. It features short anecdotes, plus photos, sketches, and other markers of what happened.

How It Works

The target audience is the new employee. After they join the company, they are sure to have heard a stream of good things about the company and the team. The team can share the Failure Book with their new member during the first lunch, to read about the mistakes that everyone has made on the job. And she'll know that when she makes her first mistake at work, she will also be asked to document it in the book for others to read about. She'll get her failure story ready before the next new team member joins. The book will grow with new stories, to assure the team members that making mistakes is okay—and to give a sense of community

NO ReHASH RULe
Nudge team members to move on

28. No Rehash Rule

 The Use Case

When you want to set a standard of shorter meetings, and to move conversations past repetitive discussions of problems.

 Team Ritual

This is an org ritual, that can be set to teams as well.

 Props

+ A symbolic thing—like a paddle, or a rubber chicken—that can add some humor to the interaction

 Difficulty Level

Medium planning ritual—there needs to be investment to set up a common rule that everyone understands.

What Is the Ritual?

If, during meetings, there's a tendency for people to circle around the same complaints or discussion topics, the No Rehash ritual is a small prompt to move past them.

The ritual is a short one, built around a No Rehash rule that you must establish in your organization. During a meeting, anyone is empowered to invoke this rule when they feel the meeting is being derailed or getting repetitive. They can hold up a "No Rehash" paddle, card, rubber chicken, or other symbol. They don't need to say the word—the action should be a signal for the people talking to come back to the point and to leave the topic that has been exhausted.

The ritual should be a short, humorous reminder to keep meetings more focused, and to let people feel they are able to cut off unproductive lines of conversation in a direct but not confrontational way.

How It Works

The key part of the ritual is to establish the common rule that people are allowed to call out a No Rehash moment, and that others will accept it without debate. It should set a culture where people are able to resolve inefficient discussions on their own, and with a common understanding that it's best to move on.

This ritual is in use in many different contexts. Brivo, a security management software provider, keeps meetings on point with its "No Rehash" rule. Employees signal to others that a topic has already been addressed by raising the "No Rehash" Ping-Pong paddle. The practice was motivated by overly long meetings, where the same decisions were made multiple times.[42] Everyone in the company was given a paddle, so that they could call out counterproductive conversations without having to go through a justification.

The software company Atlassian has a similar practice, but with a squeaky rubber chicken that stays in the middle of meeting tables. When conversations start to veer off course, anyone can squeeze the chicken to bring the group back from the tangent, to the agenda at hand.[43]

This type of ritual has also been adapted to empower community members to call out good and bad behavior around them. The former mayor of Bogotá, Colombia, Antanas Mockus, handed out 350,000 sets of cards to residents with images of thumbs-up or thumbs-down.[44] People could use the cards to signal to their fellow residents as to whether they were driving well or poorly. The cards let anyone call out someone else's driving behavior, as good or bad. The goal was to change the culture of driving by empowering people to enforce the rules. Combined with other policy interventions, traffic fatalities dropped by half in the city after the card experiment.

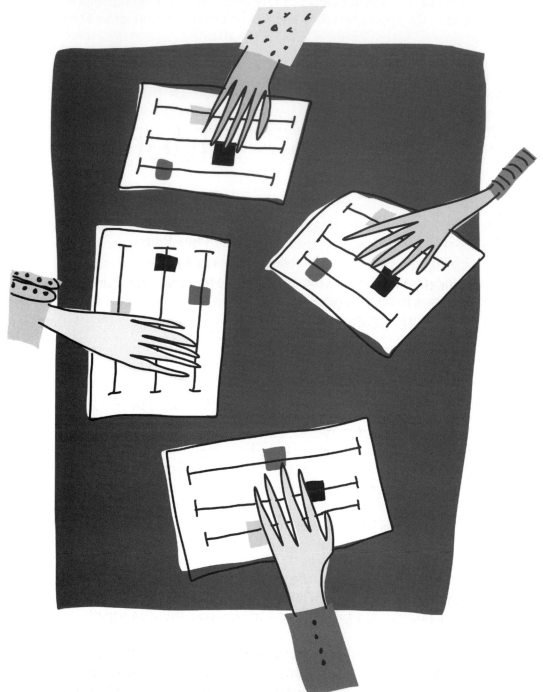

TRADE-OFF SLiders
Prevent conflicts around priorities & resources

29. Trade-off Sliders

 The Use Case

This is helpful when you want to align a team before a project, to head off conflicts that might arise.

 Team Ritual

This is a team ritual, that can be adapted for cross-teams and orgs.

 Props

+ Whiteboard or butcher paper
+ Physical sliders
+ Stickies

 Difficulty Level

Low planning ritual, that requires some material preparation.

What Is the Ritual?

When a new project is about to take off, you want to avoid future conflicts by aligning your team members. The Trade-off Sliders ritual is designed to reveal possible points of disagreement and help you prioritize together.

A team gets together, creates metrics about the project, and then physically plays with sliders to come to a common understanding of how the project priorities should be set. This ritual is good if your team members have distinct, possibly conflicting, points of view. They may struggle to get to consensus around project decisions—so this ritual can help them establish a common understanding, decide how to balance different dependencies, metrics, and decisions, before their conflicting points of view boil into arguments.

How It Works

This ritual comes from the software company Atlassian, which developed the Trade-Off Sliders as a way to build better team direction and prevent conflicts from developing.[45] They're used at the outset of a new project, when the group is in planning mode.

- Call the team together, with a big stack of large papers for each person.

- Have a conversation, in which the team decides what the top possible metrics for the project's success are. Usually these metrics include timing, scope, and budget—but let the team decide.

- Once they are set, prepare your whiteboard or butcher's paper with one bar for each metric, labeled with its name. These are the scales for your sliders. Label the ends of each scale with a value: "most negotiable" on one end, "least negotiable" on the other.

- Make tangible sliders out of sticky notes. Have one color for the first round of ranking, and another color for the final, team-wide decision.

- Give each person one slider for each metric scale. Remind them sliders are interdependent: if one goes up, another one goes down.

- Set a timer for 5 minutes for Silent Sliding. Everyone works on laying out their priorities on their own, quietly.

- Then move to Social Sliding. Let everyone reveal their slider score for every scale. Then have a brief discussion and have consensus on where to lock the slider.

- When you've reached consensus on all scales, lock in each sliding scale with the "final" sliders you prepared, in a new color.

- As you lock them all in, take a photo of the final slider metrics— and everyone around it, to recognize the moment of consensus. Shake hands, give high fives, and thank everyone for their work.

The small MOMENTs JAR
Repair a Relationship with small Appreciations

30. The Small Moments Jar

 The Use Case

When you need to strengthen appreciation of team members to each other, and prevent relationships from deteriorating.

 Team Ritual

This is a team ritual, that can also be adapted to be an individual one.

 Props

+ A large jar
+ Slips of paper, all stationed centrally

 Difficulty Level

This is a medium-planning ritual, because you must invest in continuing to leave notes to have them available when needed.

What Is the Ritual?

The Small Moments Jar helps teams build a healthy culture by instilling a habit of recognizing contributions of all shapes and sizes. When a teammate does something great—whether it's helping out on a deadline, giving a great presentation, or bringing in fancy cupcakes—another teammate can write it down on a small slip of paper and put it in the jar. The jar should be emptied regularly, such as at the end of the weekly all-hands meeting.

The Small Moments Jar should be integrated into the team's day-to-day, with a low threshold of what can be recognized. The Jar should grow week to week, with all kinds of small appreciations. This is the back-stock of positive relationship moments that can then be drawn from to keep the team strong. There can be a monthly ritual of reading through the Jar's notes.

How It Works
This ritual is an adaptation of a ritual created by Anima LaVoy (see her profile earlier in this chapter). She developed a Small Moments Jar for a more personal setting, to keep a romantic or family relationship healthy.

Here, instead of as a way to maintain strong personal relationships, it's about the relationships of team members. These often can have fluctuations between warm, cold, stressed, jealous, and collaborative. This should help balance out the more negative moments with the positive ones.

- Get a large transparent jar, and put it in a common area that's easily visible on a regular basis. Have some stickies or index cards nearby.

- Explain to the team members that they can show appreciation for one another's good work and favors by writing about it and putting it in the Jar. They should sign and date the notes that they leave.

- Ideally, people will do it regularly, and a large collection of notes will grow in it. It should be a small and easy way to recognize a good moment that happened.

- After there's at least 25 or 30 notes in the jar, you can start pulling notes out to feature them. The trigger to open them could be a weekly meeting, a team lunch, or another regular activity where everyone is together. The goal is to spotlight small, positive moments.

- You can also have weekly featured notes. The team can have a weekly draw from the Jar, like a lottery pick, with one note pulled out. The note that gets pulled can then be hung up for everyone to remember that week.

6

Community and Team Building Rituals

A community ritual can help build a shared identity through symbols, stories, and history making. These then can become reference points for people to draw on core values and feel connected.

Rituals can also be key for better meetings. They can bring humor, surprise, and meaning to routine work, to bring the best out of coworkers. They can help bring people into sync, get more productive, and build stronger empathy.

When Would You Use a Community and Team Building Ritual?

Individual
+ Create an identity to foster sense of belonging
+ Increase empathy among team members
+ Share personal stories to increase bonding

Team
+ Celebrate holidays across geographies
+ Increase team bond across offices
+ Create connections among distributed teams
+ Sync up teammates, firing their exploratory mindset

Organization
+ Create a shared memory to cultivate identity
+ Recognize civic service to the wider community
+ Break down silos among teams and departments

10 Community and Team Building Rituals

31 The Pinning Ceremony
Create a Shared Identity and a Sense of Belonging

32 The Remote Holiday Party
Celebrate to Build Shared Culture Across Geographies

33 The Global Mixtape
Build Weekly Touchstones with Music Sharing

34 Check-in Rounds
Quick Life Shares to Build Bonds

35 Three-Second Share Day
Nurture Virtual Team Bonds Through Stories

36 The Walking Meetings
Synchronize a Group While Encouraging Exploration

37 The Backstory Dinner
Share Your Personal Story Over a Special Meal

38 Our Year in Pictures
Create a Shared History Through Images

39 Citizenship Stories
Recognize the Team's Civic Impact and Engagement

40 The Bake-off Tournament
Break Down Silos with a Baking Game

The PINNING CEREMONY
CReate a shaRED IDENtity & SENSE of
BELONGING

31. The Pinning Ceremony

 The Use Case

When you need to create a shared identity, and confidence for team members who have just finished a training.

 Team Ritual

This is a team ritual that can be set for cross-teams and orgs.

 Props

+ Pins that represent your identity,
+ Script with words to repeat,
+ Pin box to hold the pins, and make the ceremony feel more official

 Difficulty Level

This is a medium-planning ritual that costs some money at the start. You need to design and order pins.

What Is the Ritual?

The Pinning Ceremony is a conclusion ritual that was developed at Stanford d.school. It gives a clear ending point—and a special, memorable moment— for a class that has usually been packed with work and tasks. It is a way to take a pause and go slowly, just as time is running out, to recognize that the class community is coming to an end.

It also is a ritual about confidence and inclusion. Many of the students have come to the class wanting to learn. They feel that they are a beginner, without a strong sense of their own design abilities. The Pinning Ceremony gives them license to have confidence that they know what design is, that they have done design work, and they are part of the d.school community.

How It Works

At the d.school, the Pinning Ceremony is held in the final session of every class. Once students have made it through the process and the course, this Ceremony is akin to a small graduation.

- The instructors take a special red velvet box and a laminated script. The team has the class come into a group circle, without telling them what is happening.

- The instructors go around the circle with the red velvet box—opening it up and going around, student by student. The red box has five different lapel pins inside: one for each of the five symbols in the d.school logo. They don't have particular meanings—but the students are allowed to speculate and say what each symbol means—and how it might be meaningful to them.

- Each student gets to choose one—but they aren't allowed to put it on yet.

- Once each person has chosen their pin, then it is time for the ceremony.

- Everyone in the circle pairs up. Their partner pins them with the pin they chose.

- During the pinning, the teachers reach out the scripted words, announcing that everyone is now officially graduated and part of the design community.

How to Adapt

The Pinning Ceremony can be adapted directly into other settings where things are "coming to an end" or where a group of people have made it through something. Having pins be the central part is a smart idea—in part because of how delicate and small they are. The physical action of having someone else pin the symbol onto you requires moving slowly, deliberately, and closely. The act of pinning makes the moment seem more momentous.

The script can be rewritten, or even shortened down to a small phrase. The key thing is that the facilitators should have some kind of official phrases to say, to make it feel more like a ceremony, and less like a usual type of interaction.

Isabel Behncke

Ph.D., Primatologist, evolutionary and behavioral scientist

Work on Rituals

Isabel's work is all about understanding the deep past. She's studied the evolutionary origin of rituals with bonobos and prehistoric societies, which can help us understand the power of rituals in our present and future.

Her work explores the context of rituals for humans—looking at them in the context of nature, compared with other social animals—and within particular communities and cultures.

She has studied humans' closest living relatives, bonobo apes, who have extraordinarily peaceful and cohesive societies, with this question: could we learn anything about their rituals (if they have them)? Bonobos managed to create a society without lethal violence, a feat that neither humans nor chimpanzees have managed yet. Following bonobos in the Congo jungle, Isabel learned that play behavior was key to their

peaceful societies. She observed that in the depths of the jungle, there existed regular instances where the animals played, at a particular time, place and context, just like human social rituals. It was not just the little ones but adults too, including—and many times led by—powerful males.

Looking at the importance of social play in our closest living relatives led Isabel to explore play and ritual in human festivals. She studied hunter-gatherer festivals in Neolithic prehistory and modern festivals like Burning Man in Nevada and Brazilian Carnival.

Learnings from Ritual Work

Isabel's research led her to a basic insight: festive ritual (and probably all ritual) is rooted in play behavior. Indeed the most important and persistent transcultural bonding rituals of humans are all rooted in play. Humans share food, share drink, make music, and engage in

synchronous behavior. The shared experience of salient emotion brings people together. Humans create spaces for ritual positive leisure. We laugh, we create, we share. This happens today throughout the world's cultures, and it was happening before we had cities and domesticated animals and plants.

Isabel named these things "social technologies." These behaviors are technologies because they're tools that routinely deliver a function: they bond communities and they enhance creativity. These are rituals that made human cultures and communities in our deep past. And as tried and tested technologies, these social technologies are what will keep building human cultures and communities into our distant futures.

To do ritual is to be human. Isabel also says: "Tell me what rituals you do and I'll tell you who you are." That goes for what kind of rituals a community or organization performs. If you examine a group's current state of rituals with an anthropologist's eye, you will learn a great deal about the unwritten codes of its culture.

The feedback loop works the other way around, too. By changing and developing new rituals, a group can change its unwritten codes. For example, you know how bonded a neighborhood or a university department is by looking at whether they organize communal feasts, with shared food, drink, and music, without being forced to do so. Likewise, if a somewhat fragmented group of people start routinely eating, drinking and music-making together, they will bond into a cohesive, more integrated social unit.

Excitement for the future of work
Isabel is excited about how we are being pushed to become wiser in order to catch up with the powers

of the technologies we are creating. These are so transformative, and we are still children with powerful tools (or weapons) in our hands. We have to up our game.

We are understandably obsessed by thinking how technology, robots and the like will change the face of being human, Isabel says. Rightly so, since many things are already changing. But it is essential that we also focus on what is not likely to change. Knowing this will keep us rooted, sane, and propel us forward.

For example, what will not change is that we are mammals, social primates. As such, we will still need to move our bodies, share food and laughter with others, experience emotion and the liberation of music, engage in frequent face-to-face interactions, social touch, nature, and playful activity. Isabel envisages many rituals changing with the face of new technologies, but she is very excited to see how many rituals, are, in their core, not changed. To be human is to adapt, but we carry our rituals since they help us, in the end, adapt together.

Isabel recommends that to create better community and culture, use social technologies (share food and drink, music making, synchronicity, shared salient emotional experiences) . As with any powerful technologies, though, they can also be misused. She recommends long-term thinking and keeping the community's interest at the center of any of these practices, and she also cautions to be aware of power-concentrating individuals. A ritual bonds, but also binds. A light saber cuts both ways!

Also, Isabel emphasizes the importance of play in creating or rolling out a new practice. Be mindful of first reducing fear in your group. Fear and stress kill "play." If you want playful humans to be open to new rituals, focus first on creating a culture where bullying and other forms of chronic fear-inducing in your people are diminished.

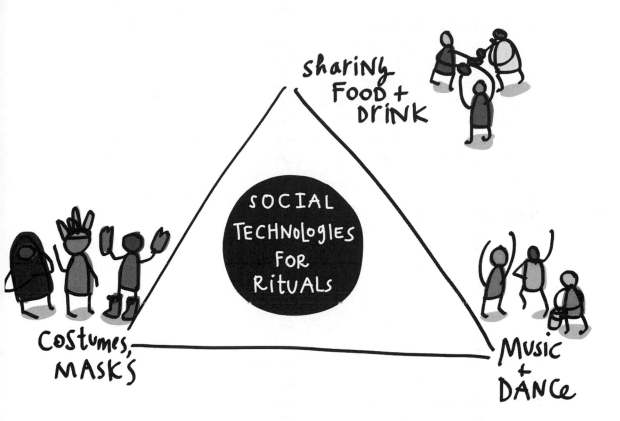

THE REMOTE HOLIDAY PARTY
Celebrate to BUILD SHARED CULTURE
Across geographies

32. The Remote Holiday Party

 The Use Case

When you want to hold celebrations across multiple teams, who don't usually get to "hang out" together.

 Team Ritual

This is a team ritual that can be set for cross-teams and orgs.

 Props

+ Camera setup
+ Video-conferencing software
+ Holiday party props as needed and desired

 Difficulty Level

Medium-planning ritual: you need to organize props, gift exchanges, and music and food as needed.

What Is the Ritual?

Holiday parties are not easy to run when team members are in many different locations. The Remote Party is a ritual meant for distributed teams, so that people can get to know each other and relax together virtually.[46] It's a way to develop work relationships beyond just connecting around work videos or conference calls.

When it's holiday season, the facilitator can set a holiday party deliberately for distributed teams. They will set a theme and schedule a party time where everyone can join comfortably, across different time zones. The celebration can be structured with in-person time to mingle, eat, and drink—and then times for virtual connection for gift exchanges, awards and thank yous, and other more formal activities.

How It Works

The goal of the Remote Holiday Party is to help people connect with one another across locations, using the videoconference technology that's usually used for work meetings to relax together.

Depending on the level of technology, there can either be videoconferences set up inside a party room—for whole groups to be calling in to other groups—or it can be individual to individual.

The facilitator should set up a shared music list, so that the different offices can play music for each other. If they want, they can also encourage people to dress up in special clothes.

A key part of the party is the gift exchange. It can be set up like a Secret Santa, where people have been randomly assigned to buy gifts for people in other offices, and have sent the gifts before the party. Then, at a set time, there can be gift openings on video, so that everyone can see the exchange. Each person, as they open the gift, gets to guess who their Secret Santa is.

Another way to do a gift exchange is through teams buying a present for specific people. For example, the software company Less Accounting does a live gift-giving ritual.[47] They have employees in six different time zones. They set up a holiday party at a certain time, when everyone logs into the party on their laptops. The company gives a set amount of money for each employee's gift.

Then, the team takes turns buying gifts for each employee. When it's a someone's turn, they turn off their audio—and everyone else gets to decide what to buy them. They buy the gift, make sure it will be delivered soon, and then move to the next person.

THE GLOBAL MIXTAPE
BUILD WEEKLY TOUCHSTONES WITH MUSIC SHARING

33. The Global Mixtape

 The Use Case

When you want to build bonds across distributed teams.

 Team Ritual

This is a team ritual that can be set for cross-teams and orgs.

 Props

+ Online music subscription that allows you to share music with others

 Difficulty Level

Medium-planning ritual: you need to create music lists and share with your team.

What Is the Ritual?

The Global Mixtape is a ritual for regularly sharing music across distributed teams, to encourage people to get to know one another and find connections outside of meetings and email. It's also about getting to find new music, and having a weekly surprise.

How It Works

Each week, a different team is in charge of setting a playlist. They play DJ, by choosing some of their favorite songs for everyone else to listen to that week. They share the playlist link and can see which songs their teammates like the most. The teams take turns to share playlists. There should be a set "release" time—a Monday morning, when the designated team sends the playlist It's a way to have a small surprise, and a new way to get to know people in other offices.

CHECK-IN ROUNDS
QUICK LIFE SHARES TO BUILD BONDS

34. Check-in Rounds

 The Use Case

When you want team members relate to each other and make empathetic connections.

 Team Ritual

This is a team ritual, can be set to pairs.

 Props

+ No props needed, just a meeting to hook into

 Difficulty Level

Low-planning ritual; you need to create the script to follow each time.

What Is the Ritual?

Many teams run "stand-up" meetings to share what work tasks people have been focusing on. Check-in Rounds are a complimentary short ritual, to nurture an environment where people feel welcome to share what else is going on in their lives. During this small ritual, at the beginning of a meeting, each person in the team shares a small status update about what's going on in their non-work life. It should just be a few sentences, and people can choose how much they want to share.

This ritual helps the team to relate to one another, build bonds, make connections. It can be a way for a team member to flag to others what else is going on in their lives.

How It Works

Check-in rounds are usually woven into an established meeting time, like a daily or weekly stand-up meeting. As people are going around to talk about what they're working on, they can be asked to also share a personal update— about their family, hobbies, weekend activities, or similar topic.

The software company Medium holds check-in rounds as a way to make sure that team members know it's okay to bring their whole self to work.[48] The goal is that these quick personal story shares can reinforce a team culture where people share their feelings, know that it is okay to be vulnerable, and build empathy between team members.

The round-robin nature can also promote inclusion, lowering the barrier for everyone in the team to speak up and talk about what's important to them. Ideally, it will help all team members feel confident to speak up throughout the meeting.

When you have a VIRTUAL TEAM, all working SEPARATELY,

DESIGNATE THE "SHARE DAY"— WHEN ALL MEMBERS WILL SHARE SCENES FROM THEIR DAY. (It could be WITH AN ASSIGNED PARTNER)

FROM MORNING TO NIGHT, THEY SHOULD CAPTURE 3 SECONDS of what they're doing + where they are, every hour.

These 3 second SNIPPETS get stitched INTO a story — & OVER THE NEXT WEEK, each meeting kicks OFF with a different PERSON'S MOVIE.

OR, it could BE SHARED DIRECTLY, CLIP BY CLIP TO YOUR PARTNER.

3 SECOND SHARE DAY
Nurture virtual tEAM BONDS THROUGH STORIES

35. Three-Second Share Day

The Use Case

When you want to help team members in different offices get to know one another.

Team Ritual

This is a team ritual.

Props

+ Smartphone with a camera
+ Folder to share pictures
+ A group messaging app

Difficulty Level

Low-planning ritual; you need to create a folder and reminders for picture taking.

What Is the Ritual?

The Three-Second Share Day ritual helps teams across geographies to connect to one another at a more personal level. It was developed in the Stanford d.school class Design Across Borders, for remote teams' collaboration.

How It Works

Team members sign up for the challenge, and then they get paired up. Throughout the specified day, people record series of three second clips of their life, with their phone's camera. They can do it at breakfast, morning commute, morning work, lunch, afternoon, and the commute home.

They send the clips to their partner, or they can stitch them together to make a video story, and share that. The partner responds with their own three second share—so they can see glimpses into each other's work lives and contexts. They can also share their video story with the whole team at meetings, so everyone can see what their day looks like.

WALKING MEETINGS
SYNCHRONIZE a GROUP while ENCOURAGING EXPLORATION

36. Walking Meetings

 The Use Case

When you want to reorient meetings to be more creative, inspiring, and energetic.

 Team Ritual

This is a team ritual.

 Props

+ No props needed. An interesting stopping destination will add more value

 Difficulty Level

Low planning ritual; you need to set up a time and destination.

What Is the Ritual?

The Walking Meetings are a simple ritual that has people walk together, along a route, when they are trying to talk through a problem or brainstorm new ideas. It shifts typical meetings or seminars from static, sedentary face-to-face gatherings to side-by-side active experiences.

A Walking Meeting is particularly powerful if a group has been in a long conference or working session, sitting with their computers in front of them for a long stretch. By changing how people are arranged, giving them a common destination, and having them walk alongside each other, the group can develop new connections and gather more inspiration during the meeting time.

How It Works

Research shows that walking boosts creativity and convergent thinking.[49] As people move in sync, their minds can also synchronize as well. Walking together can foster bonds between people. And when moving side by side, rather than facing off across a table, people can operate with less hierarchy, and develop more peer-to-peer conversations. The walking meeting should encourage people from different levels of seniority to speak to one another on a more equal plane, lowering barriers.

Walking meetings can be particularly useful when the meeting's agenda is about exploration and creativity (rather than focused, deep work).[50] The point is to allow different clusters in the meeting to diverge into different conversations, where they can explore and develop new ideas. Then the facilitator can call the clusters together at certain stops along the route, to share what they've been talking about and to rearrange as needed.

When organizing a walking meeting, there are few things to consider. The facilitator should be intentional about the walking route and timings, so that there is a basic structure to make use of the time. It's good to include a point-of-interest stop along the way, to give a sense of purpose to the group, that motivates the journey.

The ideal walking meetings will have teams cluster into pairs or trios. Just because it is outside the office, the walking meeting should still be introduced with purpose, agenda, and structure. As needed, assign roles, like a leader, a facilitator, or a scribe.

THE BACKSTORY DINNER
SHARE YOUR PERSONAL HISTORY OVER A SPECIAL MEAL

37. The Backstory Dinner

 The Use Case

Build personal links and empathy among team members, to foster stronger working relationships.

 Team Ritual

This is a team ritual.

 Props

+ Dinner
+ Projector and screen

 Difficulty Level

Medium-planning ritual; you need to set up a dinner and support the person telling their story.

What Is the Ritual?

The Backstory Dinner is a team ritual to better know where each other comes from—their family, education, values, and goals. It should be a regular event, either every week or every month. One person takes the lead at the dinner. They have an hour to present their back story, using slides, video, handouts, and whatever other materials they like. They also get to choose the dinner: their favorite food or a meal that represents their background.

During the dinner, the team gathers together in a comfortable space, like they're going to watch home movies. The person shares their life story for 30 minutes while everyone eats, and then the group can ask questions and have a conversation. Team members can discover new things about each other, and get a chance to build empathy with each other.

How it works

The Backstory Dinner has been part of Stanford's Knight and d.school fellowship programs. When a new cohort of fellows come together for a year, they take turns at the beginning of the fellowship to host Backstory Dinner nights. It's a way to help the group bond, and to appreciate all the very different backgrounds that people have come from.

This ritual has other variations. IDEO has a format that they call IDEO Stories— a Moth-like live storytelling event designed to help designers get better at storytelling. After the launch of the event, they realized it was more than a skill-building activity, it was a way to celebrate an individual's unique backstory and unite the community.[51]

At SAP Apphaus, storytelling happens in Pecha-kucha style—where 20 slides are shown for 20 seconds each (6 minutes and 40 seconds in total). This format, which keeps presentations concise and fast-paced, is a great way to have multiple speakers quickly move through their stories. Organizations could host a Pecha-kucha Backstory night, in which multiple team members can share their life story in under seven minutes.

at the end of the year, gather photos from the team + what you've been working on for the past year.

Make them into a GIANT COLLAGE that can hang as a huge poster, to preserve that history on the wall

OUr YEAR iN PicTUReS
CREATE A SHARED HiStory tHrouGH images

38. Our Year in Pictures

 The Use Case

Create a shared history with posters that live in your team's space, to commemorate what has come before.

 Org Ritual

This is an organizational ritual that can be set to teams as well.

 Props

+ A large poster or wall
+ Shared photos and images from past team work

 Difficulty Level

Medium planning ritual; someone needs to collect photos, create a poster collage, and find the best place to display them.

What Is the Ritual?

This ritual adapts a family photo wall to an organization. It creates a visual shared history of the people in the organization. At the end of the year, for a holiday party or otherwise, the team shares photos of the past year.

These images can be from work events, parties and offsites, screenshots of their daily computer life, or pictures of their work product. Everyone must share at least one photo. One person, with graphic design skills, then takes the images and assembles them into a huge collage poster. They can either print it out as a large poster to be framed and hung up, or even as a large vinyl wall covering to take up an entire wall. The visual can help form work into a narrative, and also bring a sense of family to the organization.

CITIZENSHIP STORIES
RECOGNIZE the tEAM's CIVIC IMPACT & ENGAGEMENT

39. Citizenship Stories

 The Use Case

Sharing social impact stories to remind the group of their shared values and civic responsibility.

 Org Ritual

This is an organizational ritual, that can be set to departments and teams as well.

 Props

+ A meal
+ Projector to share photos or slides

 Difficulty Level

Medium-planning ritual; someone needs to set up a specific time and location.

What Is the Ritual?

Citizenship Stories is a regular event to spotlight people in the organization who are having social impact in the community. It can also be a touchpoint to help more people join meaningful activities.

Community members who are contributing to the wider community with volunteer work, pro bono efforts, or other public service get to speak to the whole group about the project they are working on. They can highlight the purpose that motivates them, and the impact the project has.

This is a lightweight ritual to weave into other meetings, offsites, or gatherings. It can both reinforce community values in the organization and attract more people to take part in public interest work. It should show appreciation for people making the community better, educate the team about civic issues, and help people find others who share their commitments.

the BAKE-OFF TOURNAMENT
BREAK DOWN SiLOS with a BAKING GAME

40. The Bake-Off Tournament

 The Use Case

When you want to build cross-silo connections and have an event for the whole organization to bond around.

 Org Ritual

This is an organizational ritual.

 Props

+ Space to house the tournament
+ Voting material
+ Food setup

 Difficulty Level

This is a medium or high-planning ritual: someone needs to coordinate participants, as well as the events and the judging.

What Is the Ritual?

The Bake-off Tournament brings a light-hearted competition to an organization. The goal is to bring people together across silo-ed departments by having them either share their baking skills with one another, or by having them judge others' baking. The tournament sets up a weekly special event for people to come together and find out who the ultimate winner will be.

The tournament takes around 4–6 weeks, with each week being a different challenge. Everyone in the organization is welcome to participate either as a baker or as a judge. It's a way to have weekly treats, while also giving the organization a storyline: what will next week's challenge be? And who will emerge victorious?

The point is not so much having an ultimate winner, as it is getting people who normally don't work together to regularly meet, talk, and find connections.

How It Works

A large legal organization began holding a Bake-Off tournament over a summer to treat the staff with weekly baked goods, while getting people from different departments to meet and get to know one another separate and apart from day-to-day work. People who worked in the same organization for decades didn't necessarily know what others were doing. The Bake-Off was a way to break down those silos.

- Choose a 4–6 week period to hold the tournament, when it won't be too disruptive to other large commitments or holidays.

- Announce the "Bake Off" and line up people who want to participate over the course of the tournament.

- The facilitator announces the theme for each week's baking (including what ingredients are allowed) and the bakers who have signed up must bake this item—a pie, cake, pastry, cookies, macaroons, etc.—for the next judging.

- The facilitator sets up an event space for 1 hour, where each baker's food is set out anonymously, each with its own number. Everyone in the organization is welcome to drop in, and taste-test all the baked goods. They get slips of paper to write down their favorite number, and leave it in central bowl.

- At the end of the session, the facilitator tallies up the slips. The baker with the fewest votes is eliminated—and all other bakers move on to the next week.

- The tournament proceeds for the rest of the weeks. In the final judging, the baker with the most votes gets a prize—a crown, a trophy, a banner, or something else to mark their victory.

The Impact of the Bake Off Tournament

At the legal organization that set up the tournament, the impact of this ritual has been in establishing a regular social time for people to mix, talk to each other about non-work things, and learn about each others' hidden talents. During the Bake-Off Tournament, employees can make friends with others who they otherwise haven't ever spoken to. Food is a great way to bring people together, to share recipes and strategies, and to appreciate others' great skills.

Even after the one-hour weekly events, people would linger afterwards to chat, discuss their favorites, and get seconds. For weeks after the tournament, people would be sharing recipes and talking about their favorite foods. It has become a yearly event now.

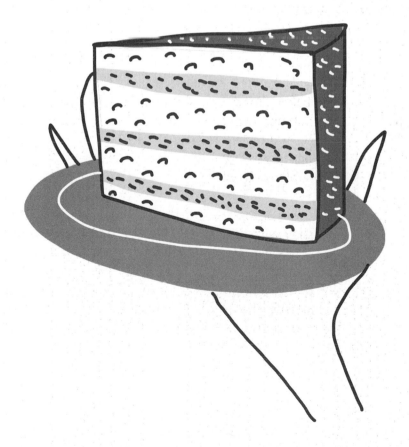

7

Org Change and Transition Rituals

Individuals, teams, and organizations have life cycles, just like in our personal lives. At work, there are arrivals, departures, mergers, advancements, divorces, retirements, demotions, and more.

During all of these transitions, rituals can be an effective way to help people deal with change. Rituals can give people back a sense of control, helping them make sense of what's happening, get used to new roles and routines, and maintain stability during times of change.

When Would You Use an Org Change and Transition Ritual?

Individual
+ Welcome a new hire into the organization
+ Celebrate the start of "real" work
+ Deal with career changes

Team
+ Achieve closure after a departure
+ Welcome new hires with the company values
+ Create an identity for a temporary team
+ Make orientations engaging

Organization
+ Have stability through mergers, acquisitions, and leadership changes
+ Get closure for departments or programs that are closing
+ Manage your org's changing direction

What Can a Transition Ritual Bring?

Supporting people as they come and as they leave

When a new employee joins an organization or gets promoted, it presents multiple opportunities for her and for the team. A thoughtful ritual can help the new employee to jumpstart building her new role, so that they can more quickly orient themselves to work here.

Welcome rituals can also make manifest the values of the organization, so that this new member can appreciate them.

When an employee is leaving the organization, rituals can give closure. Whether the exit is forced or voluntary, a transition ritual can mark the ending of a major phase in a person's life. Rather than simply ending a job, a ritual can help the person and the team move through the possibly rocky transition more smoothly.

Making a strong narrative

When big changes happen in an organization, these can destabilize an organization's core values and the stories its members tell about it. Rituals can be one way to reinforce these values through a continued narrative, and they can also help fashion new narratives to respond to a changed organization.

Aligning goals for a long journey

When a project begins, or a new team gets formed, one goal can be to align people before their long journey together. A transition ritual can sync a project or team members. It can also energize them, and help build relationships among them.

When a project or team ends, it can be time for reflection and constructive feedback. A ritual can provide structure to deal with negative emotions together, process them, and give people back control.

10 Org Change and Transition Rituals

41 A Cupcake Welcome
Surprise a New hire and Show the Company's Culture

42 The Onboarding Graduation
Celebrate New Team Members

43 Crash the Desk
A Surprise to Build Team Relationships

44 Smashing the Old Ways
Marking a Profound Change In Direction

45 Funeral for the Bygone
Grieving for Past Ways of Working to Move On

46 Mourning the Recently Left
Getting Closure After a Team Member Gets Fired or Laid Off

47 Wedding of the Orgs
Bringing Two Groups Together With Intention

48 The Name Seeker
Quickly Create an Identity For a Temporary Team.

49 The Welcome Piñata
Make a Delightful Gift for Someone Starting Off

50 The Treasure Hunt Onboarding
New Employees Build Relationships from the Start

A CUPCAKE WELCOME

surprise a new hire + show the company's culture

41. A Cupcake Welcome

 The Use Case

When a new employee has accepted a job, but hasn't yet begun—welcome them to your organization.

 Org Ritual

An organization-to-individual ritual—the org sets it up once, and then sends it to the individual employee.

 Props

+ A unique welcome kit with instructions

 Difficulty Level

Medium-to-High planning ritual; Once your org invests in designing the welcome gift and anchoring it to your key values, then it's easy to replicate.

What Is the Ritual?

When a new hire accepts your job offer, welcome them with a unique gift ritual, that represents the essence of your company's culture. Make the offer into an experience that the person will remember—something unexpected, that has a sense of delight, and that they can share with the loved ones in their life (who will also be celebrating the job offer with them).

For example, Dropbox defined "cupcakes" as one of their culture's core tenets. Accordingly, they sent a pink bakery box to each new person they offered a job to, when that person accepted the job offer. Inside the box was a make-your-own cupcake kit, so that the person could celebrate the job offer with a delicious, unique cake—and possibly share it with their loved ones.

The Cupcake Welcome Backstory

The Cupcake Kit idea was created by a Dropbox design team, who were charged with making a better welcome experience for new hires. They were guided by two big insights. Dropbox was growing rapidly, and the company needed a way to convey the culture to the new hires in a more effective way. The default way of welcoming a new hire—by throwing together a bag of leftover swag—wasn't special or thoughtful. The design team focused on how they could pass on Dropbox culture in a more deliberate way.

One of the core Dropbox values is a cupcake. It represents the company's lighthearted and delightful approach to building new software. Organizational designer Claire Pedersen took this as inspiration to make a welcome ritual. She and her team created the gift box, as well as all the ingredients to make your own cupcake that's gluten free and vegan-friendly, in the microwave.

How It Works

To make a welcome gift ritual, you first must invest in articulating the core values of your founders and company. The point of the ritual is to make special "swag" that is unique, humorous, and surprising—but most importantly, representative of some value that makes your organization unique. You can use the design process to brainstorm values. Once you identify them, then it's about choosing a symbol for the value—that you can then build your welcome gift around.

How the Welcome Gift Played Out

The team created 1000 of the Cupcake Welcome gifts. To get the ingredients and cooking exactly right, they worked closely with the company chef and had to experiment to get a quality microwave-friendly cupcake recipe.

The overall reaction to the kits was very positive. One new hire wrote a whole article about his delight at receiving the Cupcake gift, citing it as a main reason about why he joined Dropbox. Many people talked about how they gave the gift to their loved ones or made a cupcake for another.[52]

That said, the ritual is no longer in practice—as the company grew larger, they did not continue the gift-giving.

The ONBOARDING GRADUATION
CELEBRATE NEW TEAM MEMBERS

42. The Onboarding Graduation

The Use Case

After a new cohort of employees finish their training, and are ready to start "real work."

Org Ritual

This is an organizational ritual, that a team could possibly adapt to a much smaller scale.

Props

+ Food
+ Music
+ Decorations for the ceremony

Difficulty Level

This high-planning ritual requires intensive coordination to get lots of people organized and to structure the ceremony.

What Is the Ritual?

The Graduation Ceremony is a ritual that happens at the end of a new employee's training, to celebrate and recognize the hard work that the new hires went through during their first weeks at an organization. It's structured like a university graduation ceremony, though with more of a loose, party-like sensibility.

Zappos holds these ceremonies for their new classes of employees. The goal is to celebrate the new people joining the company, creating a family-like atmosphere. It also appreciates the effort that the new hires put into the first weeks of orientation, in which they have had to learn new systems, understand the company culture, and get to know so many people.

How It Works

- On graduation day, a theme is set and all employees should dress accordingly. There is a parade around campus, with music and noise makers.

- After the parade, trainees and trainers have lunch with celebratory champagne, and then the class lines up for the official ceremony.

- The trainees watch outside as the other employees come into the room with balloons, gifts, and noisemakers. At this time, other friends and family members, who have been invited by the trainees, are brought in as well to join the ceremony.

- The ceremony is orchestrated by a key group who play music and a slideshow to warm the crowd up. Then, on cue, they play Pomp and Circumstance. One of the trainers escorts the class in and guides them to their seats, to the applause of the crowd.

- The lead trainers then introduce the class of trainees. The music continues—loud and fun dance music—and each trainee's name is read out loud. The trainee comes up on stage, and gets a graduation bag.

- That trainee's team is waiting for them with confetti cannons and gifts off stage. After all of the trainees have come up, the organizers thank everyone for coming, and give them all 15 minutes to mix and mingle. Then it's time to get back to work.

The Graduation Party in Practice

The Onboarding Graduation ritual at first started small at Zappos. Trainers and trainees got into two groups at the end of each training class and competed in a trivia contest. This was happening in the classroom with a small number of people, as a more intimate ceremony.

It evolved into something bigger when Zappos moved to a downtown location. The teams invested in more structure and ceremony—to make it into more of an event. Currently, it's a full-blown professional production where the company's production group sets up music and stage lighting, and there is an orchestrated flow to the ceremony.

CRASH the DESK
A surprise to BUILD teAM RelAtionShips

43. Crash the Desk

 The Use Case

On the first day of a new employee coming into work—to get them linked into the team.

 Team Ritual

This is a team ritual—the whole team should participate, to make sure the new team member gets introduced to everyone.

 Props

+ Collect props from every member of the team, that convey a personal story to initiate conversations

 Difficulty Level

Low-cost and low-planning ritual, however, it takes the team's buy-in to make sure it happens.

What is the ritual?
Crash the Desk is an onboarding ritual for a new employee's first day of work. While the person is away from their desk on a tour or lunch, all of their new teammates leave a personal item on their desk. Then, when the person comes back and discovers their desk full of objects, they must go around with each item to find who it belongs to. When they find the right person, they can chat about what the object means.

This ritual is a welcome tour, mixed with a game. It structures a way for a new person to interact in one-on-one ways with different team members, so they can begin to build relationships and don't feel that there's a one-against-many dynamic.

How It Works

- Once the new member is introduced to the team on the first day of work, one of the team members should distract her for a short time—like going for a coffee or a short tour.

- During that time, other team members each leave one unique item on her desk. The item should somehow be related to a story about themselves. Along with the items, they leave a starter clue for the new team member, that tells her to find who each item belongs to.

- Once she comes back, she'll likely be surprised and over-whelmed with the objects on her desk. The team member should state the challenge to her: find who each item belongs to.

- There are some basic rules for the game. She cannot ask more than three hint questions to the person who has been her guide on her first day She cannot ask directly, who the item belongs to. And once she completes the game, she will be rewarded with a plant—a final gift to close the ritual and to populate her empty desk.

How it played out

This ritual was designed in one of our classes, for an innovation team at a technology company. The team has been using the ritual since the class prototyped it, but with changes. Without someone playing a shepherd, it was hard to collect all the props and get them placed on the desk.

Another evolution occurred when more than one person joined the company on the same day. In this variation, instead of a physical item, every team member wrote a personal fact on a card. When the new employee came on their first day, the team gave all the cards to him as a gift—and as a challenge. His mission was to match each card's story with the right person.

How to Adapt

You can appoint a team lead who will be responsible for collecting physical props or index cards from the other team members. You should first do a little research, to see how easy it would be for team-members to find a unique prop that tells a story. If it's too much of a challenge, have them write personal facts on index cards.

SMASHING the OLD WAYS
MARKING A PROFOUND CHANGE IN DiRECTION

44. Smashing the Old Ways

 The Use Case

When an organization changes its overall strategy, team members can physically destroy symbols of the old way.

 Org Ritual

The whole organization should participate, to make sure they are aware of these changes and take part in the transition.

 Props

+ Desktop computer (or another representation of the old way)
+ The equivalent a sledgehammer

 Difficulty Level

This medium-level cost and high-planning ritual require the team's buy-in to make sure it happens.

What Is the Ritual?

Smashing the Old Ways is a ritual ceremony for an organization to officially break from a previous strategy or a dysfunctional practice. In it, the leadership calls the organization together. It sets up a stage where some big, breakable symbol of its "old, dysfunctional ways of working" are set up. Then, when people gather together, the leaders announce: "We are going to destroy these together."

Each person gets a turn with a sledgehammer, to smash the old thing. It's like a piñata game—collectively destroying the thing until it's in smithereens. This is adapted from a Zipcar ceremony, in which employees were invited to smash desktops to reinforce the push for a mobile-first business.

It marks the transitional moment, from one large-scale company strategy to another one, in a strong way. Additionally, it creates a cathartic moment where the negative energy and anxiety about change can be released through controlled destruction. It's also a story for people throughout the organization to hold on to and tell others.

How It Works

- Zipcar was traditionally set up to work with desktop computers. When leadership decided to move to a mobile-first strategy, they want to convey this message in a more symbolic way.

- In this smashing ceremony, executives wanted to make this a significant point. People were given sledgehammers so that they could personally take up arms against the "old view" by pounding on two desktop computers.

- Smashing the old to bring in the new (literally and figuratively) created a poignant experience and instantly wrote corporate folklore that could be passed on as a symbol of exactly what was needed for the future.

How It Played Out

After they ran the smashing computers ceremony, Zipcar followed up with more activities to help bridge the transition.[53] They organized weekly member roundtables where they invited millennial customers to discuss their needs with employees. Opening up such a channel for a wide mix of employees took the effects of symbolic experience even further.

How to Adapt it

This type of intense ritual requires an aligned strategy from the leadership and a clear direction. Once it's established, the symbols and actions involved will depend on the context. It should involve some kind of physical destruction, that will have people taking an abstract mandate and making it visceral.

FUNERAL for the BYGONE
Grieving For PAST ways of WORKING to MOVE ON

45. Funeral for the Bygone

The Use Case

When the team or organization is shifting away from old organization structures and priorities, and some employees can't cope with it.

Org Ritual

The whole org should participate, to make sure that even the most recalcitrant are dealing with the changes.

Props

+ Posters, slideshows, short talks, videos, or other presentations that show what was good about the old ways

Difficulty Level

This medium-cost, high-planning ritual requires buy-in from the manager or higher-ups to make sure it happens and to get participation.

What Is the Ritual?

The Funeral for the Bygone is a ceremony to let people recognize, honor, and celebrate what is being left behind and the many people who had worked so hard on it. It is also a way to mark the changeover from this old way of working or this former team structure. The funeral can be a clear point of transition, by which people know that they are in a different era now.

This is an organizational change strategy that can been used when an organization is struggling to get employees to accept that established groups are going to be reorganized into new ones. During a lengthy change management process, many people may have nostalgia, resentment, and strong emotions about leaving behind the way things had been.

How It Works

- The organizer announces the official date when estab-lished programs, group names, or organizational structures will cease to exist -- with something new in their place.

- Together with this announcement, the Funeral event (perhaps not called a Funeral) is also announced, to let people know that there will be a gathering to mark this big organizational change.

- The organizers welcome anyone to contribute photos and stories to be featured. The whole purpose of the event is to celebrate the structures that are being phased out, and the people whose work went into them.

- On the date, the organizers set up posters and slideshows with the materials that people have sent in. They have food, low-key music, and drinks, like at a reception.

- When people have arrived, a leader plays the emcee, wel-coming everyone and restating the purpose of the event.

- People can share their stories with each other, or with the microphone, to say what they're going to miss and whom they'd like everyone to honor (like past employees).

- The emcee closes the funeral by thanking everyone.

How to Adapt It

The funeral metaphor doesn't have to be explicit in the ritual. There doesn't have to be a burial, a procession, hymns, or a eulogy (at least by name). But the ritual should function like a funeral, by bringing together a whole com-munity to recognize that an important, sad, and possibly traumatic ending has happened. It can have elements of a party, with food, music, and social-izing, but its main goal is to deal with this loss and prepare for a new era.

The ritual should involve storytelling and sharing. It's about giving people the chance to tell their stories and explain their experiences and to show appre-ciation for the good things that have come before. It should also let people process their grief and anxiety about moving on in a collective way, and not sweep the old ways away without celebrating them in a shared ceremony.

MOURNING the RECENTLY LEFT

Getting CLOSURE after A TEAM MEMBER gets FIRED or LAID OFF

46. Mourning the Recently Left

 The Use Case

When one of your teammates gets laid off or fired, and you want closure.

 Team Ritual

The whole team's participation is preferable to make sure there is closure.

 Props

+ Sticky notes
+ Pen
+ Box
+ Shredder, or a safe burning setup

 Difficulty Level

This low-level planning ritual requires the team's buy-in to make sure it happens.

What is the ritual?

This ritual deals with a major disruption—when someone is fired from a team—to have catharsis and closure. The team moves through a debrief, about what they won't miss and what they will miss about the newly departed team mate. They each claim one of the "Will Miss" things, and they burn the box of the "Won't Miss" ones.

A team in our class created this ritual as a way to address a particularly upsetting transition, by giving remaining team members a way to talk with each other about what happened in a constructive way that can possibly reenergize them after an unexpected fractious experience. It can also help them show appreciation to a departed team member, despite problems that arose.

WEDDING of the ORGS
Bringing two groups together with intention

47. Wedding of the Orgs

The Use Case

When two companies merge, or when a large company acquires a new company.

Org Ritual

This is an organization-to-organization ritual that can be set to merging teams as well.

Props

+ A set of vows
+ Marriage certificate
+ Flowers
+ Music
+ Cake and drinks

Difficulty Level

This high-level planning ritual requires detailed design of the event and buy-in from new team members.

What Is the Ritual?

The Wedding of the Orgs is a ritual for two organizations to officially mark their merger (or acquisition). Instead of having a "normal" transition, with a formal email to mark the combination of the organizations, this ritual marks a special occasion with a more creative, collaborative event that draws on the rich ritual details of weddings.

The design agency IDEO developed this ritual when their organization was formally combining with another group. To mark this, they made a chapel in their kitchen, with flowers, an oversized marriage certificate, and a ceremony with the two companies' representatives walking down the aisle, signing the certificates, and shoving cakes into each others' mouths.

The companies came together to design the event within 24 hours, in order to make the acquisition feel human-centered and extraordinary. The notions of "acquisition" and "merger" can feel impersonal and threatening. This ritual was meant to make it feel like the start of new lives together as a family.

How it works

- Choose an officiant from each company who will lead the ceremony and make sure that there's a clear script to follow.

- Someone should be in charge of making a "chapel" in a kitchen or other large space. Get flowers, two banks of chairs with an aisle in between, and music to play. Try to make it look as celebratory as possible.

- Prepare "vows" to be said. This can be done by leaders or the group, to represent the values and relationship they want to have. For example, borrow from IDEO's example: "We, on behalf of [company], take you, [other company], to be our partners in work. We promise to cherish our friendship, honor you and your contributions, and we will work to make you successful today, tomorrow, and as long as the world requires our services."

- Make a marriage certificate that both companies' members can sign. Make a huge poster of it and hang it in the chapel.

- Invite all people involved in the merger, to participate in the ceremony. They sit down and listen to the music, and then the company representatives walk down the aisle as the music swells.

- The officiant leads the representatives in reading out their vows, saying "I do" to make it official, and they sign the certificate.

- Then they cut the cake and smash it into each others' faces. Everyone claps, pops open champagne, and stays around to eat, drink, and get to know one another.

How to Adapt

This ritual was designed within IDEO's Chicago office when they were coming together with a data science company. To adapt it, it's worth making the ceremony, vows, props, and certificate fit with your own values and worries about the merger or acquisition you're holding the ritual for. This means that each organization should reflect on what they are nervous about with the transition. It's a fragile point in each organization's life cycle, because there will be so much change and possible loss of identity.

The Wedding ritual should focus on how to navigate the strong emotions that people will be feeling, and to direct the relationships to the better future that each side wants. To adapt the ritual, each side should write its vows to lay out what that better future is, and to also acknowledge what they're worried about, to be able to address it.

The actual ceremony can also weave in the organizations' cultural practices: favorite foods, music, symbols, and in-jokes. The goal is to make the ceremony a bridging event, to bring along each organization's culture, share it with the new members, and reinforce that the transition does not mean a total loss of identity.

Annette Ferrara

Experience Director
IDEO Chicago

Work on Rituals
Annette is an experience director at the design agency IDEO, in its Chicago office—where she has developed many rituals and other culture-building strategies.

Annette and her team work to make sure employees feel safe to experiment, that they feel connected to the others around them, and that they are supported to do creative work. To do this they have invented all kinds of rituals, several of which are profiled in this book, along with others like:

IDEO Stories
Sad Iron Chef Contest
Studio Awards Party
Creative Excellence Salons
Roof Deck Movie Night
Pinewood Derby
Fancy Friday

The list goes on from there, with games, special meals, curious meetings, and holiday parties. The team loves creating rituals to develop a stronger and more creative culture.

Learnings from Rituals at Work
Annette says that rituals can be ways to help creative professionals go through different phases—like "nesting" and "stretching." Rituals offer safe, stable spaces and practices. These ease the daily transitions at work when people have to focus in on detailed work and then switch over to social engagements or taking on new challenges. Rituals can also stretch people and their creativity so their skills don't atrophy.

Annette's team uses the design process to create their events and rituals. They look for behaviors that have naturally grown up in the workplace.

For example, people were making sad sandwiches out of leftover materials in the office fridge. They took this behavior and turned it into a contest, to transform humble materials from the office kitchen into excellent dishes. It evolved into an office ritual, the Sad Iron Chef contest, codifying it into a part of their culture.

Their team also works to make rituals inclusive, incorporating as many people as they can. It's about letting people take leadership and adapt the activities with their own vision and skills.

About the Future of Work

The team at IDEO works on workplace culture as a way to help people find more meaning and community.

If people are losing other social network supports that used to be provided by nuclear families or organized religion, work takes on more important roles in helping people find purpose.

If this continues, work culture will be more important to people's social health—how they feel connected, important, and supported. There needs to be more thought given about how to build this more supportive work culture, to ensure that people can thrive in these new dynamics.

THE NAME SEEKER
Quickly create AN IDENTITY FOR a temporary teAM

48. The Name Seeker

 The Use Case

When a project happens across cross-functional teams, and people who don't normally work together must sync up.

 Team Ritual

This is a team ritual.

 Props

+ Books to pick name ideas from

 Difficulty Level

This is a low-cost and low-planning ritual—it just takes the team's buy-in to make sure it happens.

What Is the Ritual?

Name Seeker is a naming ritual for a temporarily-formed project team. When people come together for a short collaboration, often it's hard to get them to feel like they share an identity, or to get them to invest in the team.

This ritual has new teammates kick off their collaboration by picking a name together using their favorite books. They randomly choose words from the books, and then work together to make them into a name and form a shared story around the name.

The key of the Name Seeker ritual is to get teams to create a name together, that will not last forever but that will work for as long as the temporary team is operating. The ritual brings some randomness into the decision, so that it is not about individuals competing for the best name. The group can react together to what the ritual produce, and they can work with the random prompts to create something meaningful: their first team decision.

How It Works

The Name Seeker ritual is a lightweight one, that should be a fun, creative, and surprising exercise for the newly formed team.

- When a team has been formed, invite them for a kickoff meeting—and ask them to bring their favorite book.

- At the meeting, have three people volunteer to go first. They open their favorite book to a random page, put their finger on a word randomly—all without looking.

- They should write this word down on a piece of paper.

- Now have another three people do the same—open their book, randomly choose a word, and write it down.

- Once the team has around ten words, lay them all out in the center or on a board. Now the team needs to pick from these—possibly mashing them together, or riffing off of them—to make a team name.

- Write the team name out on the board or a large poster board. Have the team now decide on what the logo should be, that fleshes out this name, and helps explain the backstory.

- Finally, write down the three to five key principles of this team. This can weave back to the name and the logo, to make a more coherent identity. All of this work—the name, logo, and principles—can then be carried into the team's space to mark their new identity.

Figure out your company's MASCOT — the THING that Represents your CORE VALUES + TRAITS

MAKE That THING INTO A PIÑATA That ALL New hires WILL get ON THEiR Desk ON the First Day OF WORK

They CAN Break it OPEN, & FIND A WELCOME PResent— DINNER With Their LoVED ONes TO celeBRate The New JoB.

THE WELCOME PIÑATA
Make a DELIGHTFUL GIFT for SOMEONE starting OFF

49. The Welcome Piñata

 The Use Case

When a new hire comes in for the first day of work.

 Org Ritual

This is an organization-to-individual ritual.

 Props

+ Unique symbol of the company or mascot, made into a piñata
+ Surprise gift inside

 Difficulty Level

This is a high-planning ritual: it requires investment to create the small piñata gifts.

What Is the Ritual?

The Welcome Piñata is a small onboarding ritual that welcomes a new person to the team with a playful surprise gift. Rather than the usual welcome swag—a coffee cup, a tote bag, or a notebook—the piñata is a delightful and interactive gift that should represent the organization's identity.

How It Works

The company should choose its mascot, or another symbol that it wants to project. It should be something that represents the values of the organization. Once that symbol is chosen, then piñata versions of it should be made, and filled with candies, mints, or other treats. Whenever a new person joins the company, a piñata should be waiting on their desk as a surprise gift. They can break it open to find the treats—and perhaps also a gift certificate to cover a meal with their loved ones to celebrate their new job.

THE TREASURE HUNT ONBOARDING
NEW EMPLOYEES BUILD RELATIONSHIPS from the START

50. The Treasure Hunt Onboarding

 The Use Case

When a new hire comes in for their first day at work.

 Org Ritual

This is an organization-to-individual ritual, that can be set for teams.

 Props

+ Treasure hunt map
+ Clues
+ Awards

 Difficulty Level

Once your organization invests in designing the treasure hunt, then it is easy to replicate.

What Is the Ritual?

On the first day of a person's employment, often a team member leads them around the space to introduce them to all their new co-workers. This ritual adapts this practice into a game, with a map that lays out clues for all the stops, and a special prize at the end as a payoff. It was designed by a technology company and students in one of our recent Stanford classes.

The new employee is given a Treasure Map on their first day of work. They have to find their way from one stop to the next using the map's clues. They can ask others for help, and when they come to the right place, then the co-worker there will welcome them and give them more clues.

Once the person finishes the Hunt, they get a welcome gift. The Treasure Hunt should make the first day more engaging, so the person gets to know their co-workers in a more memorable way and have a supportive structure on a day that could be overwhelming.

PART THREE

Designing Rituals with and for Your Teams

8

A Short Guide to Designing Rituals

After reading about other rituals, perhaps you are interested in creating one that would fit your context and goals. We encourage you to experiment with ritual design, to imagine how your work life and relationships could be better.

We have designed rituals over the past four years in our workshops and classes. The basic process of creating a new ritual has three big phases: Discovery, Design, and Deployment.

In the Discovery phase, you explore potential moments, inspirations, and intentions that could be at the heart of your ritual. Then in the Design phase you switch to experimenting with various elements to create the right experience. In the Deployment phase, you think more strategically, about how to roll out your ritual so that it is nimble, low-barrier, and likely to be adopted and adapted by your community.

Step 1

Discover: **Set Your Intention**
Why create a ritual?

Set an intention to be at the heart of your ritual. What is the point that you want it to make, or the emotion you want it to embody? An intention can be based on your or your organization's values, beliefs, goals, motivations, or aspirations.

For example it could be about being a better colleague, inspiring more creativity on your team, or creating a sense of welcome to new employees.

Step 2

Discover: **Find a Hook**
What's the context trigger: specific time, people, and place?

A trigger is an opportunity moment around which you can build a strong ritual. Some triggers might be when a colleague gets promoted, a product is released, a team kicks off a project, a conflict arises, or a product fails. Once you identify the trigger context, pick a specific situation within this larger context to anchor your ritual. It could be at a weekly meeting, at a coffee break in the lounge, or at a goodbye dinner. This specificity of time and place will make your ritual more likely to stick.

Step 3

Design: **Ideate**
What are possible elements of your ritual?

Brainstorm ritual ideas that would bring your intention to life. Ideally, you can do this with others, to combine your insights. To get inspired, try ritual-specific prompts that draw on what we know from scholarship about what works, like drawing from Isabel Behncke's work on social technologies:

Prompt 1: Share food and drink
Prompt 2: Use special costumes—especially things on your head
Prompt 3: Involve rhythm and movement

For more, use our app Ideapop via our website http://ritualdesignlab.org.

Step 4

Design: **Define a Symbolic Prop or Act**
What Makes Your Ritual Special?

After a first round of brainstorming, see if there's any key moment and symbolic prop or act that you can build your ritual around. There are some exercises that can help you iterate upon your initial ideas.

Iteration 1: Add a Magic Prop—give extra powers to a prop for your ritual. For example, for an athlete you could give the sneaker a special aura.

Iteration 2: Add a Reward moment—of physical, emotional, or social payoff

Iteration 3: Add a Catharsis moment—that would be a particular action to release negative emotions and energy.

Step 5

Design: **Refine It into an Arc**
How does your ritual unfold?

A good ritual has a narrative arc with a beginning, middle, and end. Take your selected idea, and make it into a full arc. You can do this with storyboarding, drawing out the new ritual in steps. Try to refine the ritual based on the ritual principles mentioned earlier in the book.

Principle 1: Does your ritual have a *je ne sais quoi* quality?
Principle 2: Does your design work toward your intention?
Principle 3: Does it carry symbolic value, and go beyond practicality?
Principle 4: Does it have room for evolution: can you add or subtract things based on the needs of your participants?

Step 6

Deployment: **Act Out**
How will people perform your ritual?

Now act it out, to test whether the ritual works in practice. This will be like a second round of brainstorming—but less intellectual and more physical. By acting it out—and taking it as an improv project, in which you can change exactly what you're doing—you can refine your ritual into something that feels comfortable, playful, and meaningful.

Hopefully you have a partner or two to act it out with. Try to play off each other's physical actions—repeating it until you sync up. Repeat different variations of words, and then objects. See what sticks and refine.

Step 7

Deployment: **Codify**
How can you make the ritual into a "thing" that has an effect?

Use the ritual canvas template, drawn above and available at http://ritu-aldesignlab.org, to codify your ritual. Define the essential script and props, and detail the arc's beginning, middle, and end. List your intention and context trigger to make it complete.

When you want to roll it out into practice, use the Ritual Roll Out guide in Chapter 2 to think about how best to involve others and scale up your idea into regular practice. Be open to your designed ritual being adapted. It's an experiment that may fail to catch on in its original plan, but people can improve upon to make it the right fit for their work life.

Endnotes

1   Amy Adkins, "Employee engagement in U.S. Stagnant in 2015", https://news.gallup.com/poll/188144/employee-engagement-stagnant-2015.aspx

2   Rafael Nadal, *Rafa*. New York: Hyperion, 2011.

3   Soren Kaplan, "Zipcar doesn't just ask employees to innovate, it shows them how", *Harvard Business Review*, Feb 1, 2017.

4   James Heskett, *The Culture Cycle: How to shape the unseen force that transforms performance*. Upper Saddle River, NJ: Pearson FT Press, 2015.

5   Kursat Ozenc, "Modes of Transitions: Designing Interactive Products for Harmony and Wellbeing," *Design Issues*, Vol. 30, No, 2, 2014.

6   Kursat Ozenc and Margaret Hagan, "Ritual Design: Crafting Culture and Designing Meaning for Organizational Change," AHFE International, 2016.

7   Emile Durkheim, *The Elementary Forms of the Religious Life*, trans. J.W.Swain, London: Allen and Unwin, 1957.

8   Clifford Geertz, *Interpretation of Cultures*, New York: Basic Books, 1973, at p. 112.

9   Nicholas Hobson et al., "The Psychology of Rituals: An Integrative Review and Process-Based Framework," *Personality & Social Psychology Review*, 2017.

10 Carmen Nobel, "The Power of Rituals in Life, Death, and Business," *Working Knowledge*, Harvard Business School, June 2013.

11 Alison Wood Brooks et al., "Don't stop believing: Rituals improve performance by decreasing anxiety," *Behavior and Human Science*, 2016.

12 Michael I. Norton and Francesca Gino, "Rituals Alleviate Grieving for Loved Ones, Lovers, and Lotteries," *Journal of Experimental Psychology: General*, Vol. 143, No. 1, 2014, at p. 266–272.

13 Daniel McGinn, *Psyched Up: How the Science of Mental Preparation Can Help You Succeed*, Penguin Random House, 2017.

14 Daniel McGinn, "Why You and Your Colleagues Need a Group Ritual," *Time*, 2017.

15 Kathleen D. Vohs, et al. "Rituals Enhance Consumption," *Psychological Science*, Volume 9, Sept 24, 2013, at pages 1714–21.

16 Allen Ding Tian, et al. "Enacting Rituals to Improve Self-Control," *Journal of Personality and Social Psychology*, Vol. 114, 2018, at p. 851–876.

17 Mason Currey, *Daily Rituals: How Artists Work*, New York: Knopf, 2013.

18 Michaela Schippers and Paul van Lange, "The Psychological Benefits of Superstitious Rituals in Top Sport," ERIM Report Series Reference, 2005.

19 Lisa Schirch, *Ritual and Symbol in Peacebuilding*, Kumarian Press, 2005.

20 Chip and Dan Heath, *The Power of Moments*, New York: Simon & Schuster, 2017, at p. 17–39.

21 Herbert Simon, *Sciences of the Artificial*, Cambridge, MA: MIT Press, 1969.

22 This drawing was inspired by W. Sluckin, D. J. Hargreaves and A. M. Colman," Novelty and Human Aesthetic Preferences", 2000.

23 "Peek Inside the Annual Flipboard Mockathon," https://about.flipboard.com/inside-flipboard/peek-inside-the-annual-flipboard-mockathon/.

24 MIT's Design Mad Libs, https://www.media.mit.edu/articles/in-a-creative-rut-try-mit-s-mad-libs-for-designers/.

25 IdeaPop is an iOS app, at Ritual Design Lab, https://ritualdesignlab.org.

26 Jonathan D. Rockoff, "Celebrating Failure in a Tough Drug Industry," *The Wall Street Journal*, March 2017.

27 Caroline Copley and Ben Hirschler, "For Roche CEO, celebrating failure is key to success," *Reuters*, September 2014.

28 Laura Miner, "Founding and Designing Pinterest's Internal Conference: Knit Con," http://lauraminer.com/knit-con/.

29 Francesca Gino, "Need More Self-Control? Try a Simple Ritual," *Scientific American*, August 2018.

30 See examples of Amp-Up rituals at notes 2, 13, 14 and 18.

31 Paul Levy, "Seeing Past the Checklist," *Athena Insight*, January 2017.

32 Camille Sweeney and Josh Gosfield, "11 Simple Tips For Having Great Meetings From Some Of The World's Most Productive People," *Fast Company*, June 2013.

33 Marshall Goldsmith, "Six daily questions for winning leaders," *Dialogue*, Q1 2017.

34 Kasey Fleisher Hickey, "How to take back your productivity with No Meeting Wednesday," *Wavelength*, https://wavelength.asana.com/workstyle-no-meeting-wednesdays.

35 Jason Fried, "Why work doesn't happen at work," at TEDxMidwest, October 2010.

36 Rich Karlgaard and Michael S. Malone, *Team Genius*, Harper Collins, 2015.

37 Lisa Maulhardt, "Advice for new leaders in your first 100 days," https://www.sypartners.com/insights/tips-for-new-leaders/.

38 Alice Truong, "The oddball ways tech companies welcome you on your first day of work," *Quartz*, March 2015.

39 The Doctor Is In work is licensed with express permission from Atlassian under a Creative Commons Attribution-NonCommercial-ShareAlike 4.0 International License.

40 Matter-Mind Studio, "Design Poetics," https://www.mattermindstudio.com/designpoetics.

41 "How Airbnb is Building its Culture Through Belonging," *Culture Amp Blog*, https://blog.cultureamp.com/how-airbnb-is-building-its-culture-through-belonging.

42 Dom Price, "6 Meeting Hacks (and 1 Weird Tip) That Instantly Boost Your Credibility," *Inc.*, Jan. 2018.

43 Jurgen Spangl, "Want better meetings? Meet Helmut, the rubber chicken," *Atlassian Blog*, April 2017.

44 Maria Cristina Caballero, "Academic turns city into a social experiment," *The Harvard Gazette*, March 2004.

45 See https://www.atlassian.com/team-playbook/plays/trade-off-sliders. This work is licensed with express permission from Atlassian under a Creative Commons Attribution-NonCommercial-ShareAlike 4.0 Intl. License.

46 Lauren Hamer, "How to Make Remote Team Celebrations Memorable & Merry," *Office Ninjas*, https://officeninjas.com/remote-team-celebrations-and-work-holidays/.

47 Margaret Littman, "Beyond Secret Santa: Holiday Traditions That Build Teams," *Entrepreneur*, Dec. 2013.

48 Jennifer Dennard, Check-in Rounds: A Cultural Ritual at Medium, *3 Min Read*, Aug. 2016, https://blog.medium.com/check-in-rounds-a-cultural-ritual-at-medium-367fbcf15050.

49 Marily Oppezzo and Daniel L. Schwartz, "Give your ideas some legs: The positive effect of walking on creative thinking," *Journal of Experimental Psychology: Learning, Memory, and Cognition*, Vol. 40, 2014, at p. 1142–1152.

50 Russell Clayton, Christopher Thomas, and Jack Smothers, "How to Do Walking Meetings Right," *Harvard Business Review*, Aug. 2015.

51 Annette Ferrara, "Why workplace culture matters and how to build a good one," IDEO Blog, June 2018.

52 Kurt Varner, "Why I am joining Dropbox," *Medium*, July 2016. Also see the project at Claire Pedersen's website, http://clairepedersen.com.

53 See Kaplan, 2017, at note 3.

Acknowledgments

This book would not be possible without the help of our family, friends, and colleagues.

We would like to thank our families who live in the U.S. and in Turkey, with special thanks to Kerem and Teoman.

Thank you to the Stanford d.school community, who inspired us to share our work with the wider community. We thank our students and partnering organizations at SAP, Microsoft, and Stanford Center for Design Research. We would also like to thank our collaborators who have taught with us before, including David Sirkin, Isabel Behncke, Defne Civelekoglu, and Professor Anne Mundell.

We thank Professor Richard Buchanan, Professor John Zimmerman, and Professor Lorrie Cranor for supporting the designing for transitions research at Carnegie Mellon, which inspired the work on ritual design.

Thanks to Reina Takahashi in supporting the design of our book. And thanks to Justin Lokitz who opened us up to the art of the possible.

Thank you to all our interviewees: Annette Ferrara, Anima LaVoy, Ayse Birsel, Cipriano Lopez, Dom Price, Isabel Behncke, Laura Miner, Lilian Tong, Marshall Goldsmith, and Nick Hobson for their openness, curiosity, and great work.

And thank you to the community who showed up at the first Ritual Design Summit at Stanford in May 2018, for their feedback and ideas.

Finally, thank you to Hamide, Metin, and Bekir for all their support while writing and drawing the book.

Authors

Kürşat Özenç, Ph.D.
Strategic Design Consultant, SAP Labs, Lecturer at Stanford University d.school

Kürşat Özenç is a designer and an innovation consultant. He creates tools and services for experts and everyday people. He leads the Ritual Design Lab initiative at Stanford d.school, where he runs experiments with students and partner organizations on personal, team and human-robot rituals. He also teaches service design at the d.school.

His work on rituals has appeared in Atlantic Magazine and on the Canadian Public Radio. He holds degrees from Carnegie Mellon University, Sabanci University, and Middle East Technical University. He's originally from the Cappadocia region, Turkey.

Margaret Hagan, Ph.D.
Director of Legal Design Lab, Stanford University Law School, Lecturer at d.school

Margaret Hagan is a lawyer and a designer. She teaches at Stanford Law School and d.school, where she runs the Legal Design Lab, that does research and development for improving people's access to the justice system.

She holds degrees from the University of Chicago, Stanford University, Queen's University Belfast, and Central European University. Along with her studies, she is also an avid drawer. She is originally from Pittsburgh, Pennsylvania.

Index

WANT MORE?

We have reading lists, More examples of rituals, & resources to help you design your own Rituals (like our App "IdeAPOP") at our website

https://ritualdesignlab.org

COME SHARE WITH US YOUR RITUALS FOR WORK, TOO. WE'D LOVE TO SEE THEM.